Pantomime Hero

Pantomime Hero

Jimmy Armfield

Memories of the man
who lifted Leeds
after Brian Clough

Ian Ridley

FOOTBALL
SHORTS

**FOOTBALL
SHORTS**

First published by Pitch Publishing
and Floodlit Dreams, 2023

Pitch Publishing
9 Donnington Park,
85 Birdham Road,
Chichester,
West Sussex,
PO20 7AJ
www.pitchpublishing.co.uk
info@pitchpublishing.co.uk

A CIP catalogue record is available for this book
from the British Library.

ISBN 978 1 80150 483 6

Typesetting and origination by Pitch Publishing

Printed and bound in Great Britain by TJ Books, Padstow

His life was gentle, and the elements

So mixed in him that nature might stand up

And say to all the world: 'This was a man.'

Julius Caesar, Act V Scene V

NOTES AND ACKNOWLEDGEMENTS

WELCOME TO this first book in the Football Shorts series, an exciting partnership between Pitch Publishing and my own Floodlit Dreams company.

During the various lockdowns of recent years, I sometimes felt like just a short sporting read, rather than a long, weighty one, but found such books hard to come by. It got me thinking... and fortunately Jane Camillin at Pitch Publishing thought it was a good idea too when I went to her with it. Thus am I hugely grateful to them for backing this idea, entering into a partnership and putting Pitch's deep practical knowledge of producing a wide range of great sports books at the disposal of this project.

The aim is to publish three books a year by fine writers telling engaging personal tales of the football world, to entertain and inform. They are reads to fit into pockets and bags – and to fit into busy schedules too. However, when it comes to some of the writers we have lined up, I suspect you'll be tempted to read them avidly in one go.

After *Pantomime Hero*, the spring of 2023 will see Jane Purdon, former chief executive of Women in Football, share her remarkable story of a life in the (predominantly women's) game, in which she worked for both the Premier League and her home-city club Sunderland. She will detail the joyful and long-overdue re-emergence of women's football encapsulated by the Lionesses' European Championship win of 2022, and examine the progress ahead of the World Cup in Australia and New Zealand.

Then in the autumn, Andy Hamilton, the celebrated comedy writer and performer, will tell his charming but incisive tale of growing up supporting Chelsea. Set in the wider context of how the game and his club have changed along with his feelings and attitudes, it will be full of his trademark wit, but also contain some very astute observations and judgements on life and football.

On a personal note, I am delighted to be kicking off and then curating the series. Later in 2023 we will be announcing another three great writers' books for the following year.

My thanks for the production of this book go to those who have helped me with it, especially Duncan and John Armfield, Jimmy's sons, who have generously offered deeply intimate insights of their father and their relationship with him. I am also grateful to Don Warters and Paul Reaney for their recollections of Jimmy's time at Leeds United. Further gratitude too, goes to Duncan Olner for the cover design, to Alex Ridley for establishing our website, www.football-shorts.co.uk, to my partner in Floodlit Dreams Seth Burkett and to Charlotte Atyeo, editor extraordinaire.

Huge gratitude, too, to two great men, Bill W and Bruce Lloyd, who have been saving my life one day at a time for more than 30 years. Above all, my deepest thanks go to another great man: Jimmy Armfield himself. You will read conversations between us at points in this book. This is because when they were over, I always made notes – partly since he usually had pearls of wisdom to impart that I wanted to retain and partly since I knew that one day I'd want to write a book about him.

This one is about memories of, and a friendship with, one of the most humble and remarkable men ever to grace English football. It is built around an astonishing episode in the history of the game, which reveals the essence of Jimmy as a human being and how he treated and inspired people following his taking over as manager of Leeds United from Brian Clough after 44 fabled, acrimonious days in 1974. I hope you enjoy the book, and indeed this series.

Ian Ridley

1

MY BOYHOOD footballing hero was Jimmy Greaves of Tottenham Hotspur and England. Dashing, handsome, prolific scorer of goals, he was everything I wanted to be when I grew up. Then when I became a man, or rather a middle-aged man, and finally saw that there was more to life than sheer sporting ability (though I never lost my admiration for Greaves nor awe at his talent), my hero became Jimmy Armfield. Yes, Jimmy A was a footballer who loved the game and its people. Yet, beyond that he was a rounded human being with an astonishing array of interests, one who loved life in all its guises and with all its vagaries, and people in general.

Never meet your heroes, goes the old adage. In Jimmy Armfield's case, I will be eternally grateful that I did. I like to think that in the last quarter of his life he might even have considered me a friend; I certainly did him. I will feel forever blessed to have had his example of humanity at its most generous of spirit. Football isn't always kind to its stalwarts, but its propensity for fostering bitterness due to that treatment rarely, if ever, assailed him. To be at his moving, magnificent funeral in February 2018, as one of the few journalists for whom room was found, was to be reminded through tribute after tribute, listening to friend after friend, of the warmth and admiration people had for him. In all my time around the sport, whenever Jimmy's name came up I never heard a single bad word spoken about him from anyone. Some achievement in a sport of politics and personalities, intrigue and insecurity.

But first, rather than final, things first. As a boy, though obsessed with Jimmy G, I was aware of Jimmy A – except that, in all honesty, as a right-back, he did not especially interest this budding forward. No, what I loved was that tangerine – not orange, tangerine – shirt of Blackpool FC in which he was often pictured, as their marquee player, in the magazines of the

1960s that I bought with my Saturday pocket money: *Goal*, *Charles Buchan's Football Monthly* and such. They seemed to abound then, even before a new generation of the likes of *Shoot!* and *Match!* arrived. Jimmy would be kneeling, hand on ball, smiling widely at the camera, or essaying a staged volley with the Bloomfield Road terraces in the background. Blackpool were still a big club then, a legacy of the Stanley Matthews era, before the abolition of the maximum wage in 1961 gradually meant that the bigger-city clubs with larger fan bases could more afford the better players. The rule change of 1983 to allow home clubs to keep their own gate revenue favoured the bigger clubs more too than the Blackpools, who no longer saw a 25 per cent share from, say, Manchester United's support, cementing the change in the game's landscape.

In my own seaside home of Weymouth in Dorset as a seven-year-old becoming football daft – mainly through those magazines and the *Daily Mirror* that my parents took – I was also aware of the 1962 World Cup. I knew that Jimmy was the England captain and even though none of it was live on TV, just some black-and-white highlights that were on too late for a primary school boy, I noted that he was voted the best right-back in the tournament.

A year later, he captained England against the Rest of the World at Wembley, pride on his beaming face as he led out the team alongside his opposite number, the great Argentine, and serial European Cup winner with Real Madrid, Alfredo Di Stefano. The photograph would grace the front cover of Jimmy's 2004 autobiography, *Right Back to the Beginning.*

Quite probably, Jimmy would have been the England captain at the 1966 World Cup, and won many more than his 43 caps, but for a serious groin tear that kept him out of action for almost two years between tournaments. Bobby Moore, of course – pictured just behind Jimmy in that Rest of the World match line-up – was Alf Ramsey's choice as successor. By the time Jimmy was fit again, George Cohen had been installed at right-back and Jimmy could not win back his place. At that time, as an 11-year-old, I was more concerned – tearfully mortified actually – that Jimmy Greaves could not get back into the side for the final after an injury in a group game.

The reactions of the two men that day of the 1966 final could not have been more different. Looking back at footage and stills, poor Jimmy G is painfully sad and silent, even sulky and sullen, unengaged with it all despite the tense excitement of the endgame as he stands by the England bench. 'The loneliest man in Wembley Stadium that day,' he later said. How huge the pain must have been: the man the country most expected to score the goals that would secure the 12-inch golden trophy missing out on English football's greatest day.

Jimmy A, meanwhile, is a smiling participant, though he hadn't played a minute of the tournament. Dressed in his 'lucky' red V-neck sweater and grey polo neck, despite it being the last day of July, Jimmy raises his arms at the final whistle and looks to the heavens before embracing the unemotional Ramsey. The perfect squad member, the leader of the reserve XI, the man Ramsey had asked to look after the reserves – whom Jimmy would describe as 'my lot' – and to keep their spirits up.

This is not to judge either man; they were just different people with different natures who approached their struggles from often opposite directions.

The next day, the nation still *en fête*, Jimmy G hid himself away – part through melancholy, part through not wanting to inflict that on others – and would quickly escape the country for a holiday as the rest of the players basked in the glory. While the following season he bounced back with Spurs as an FA Cup winner and the First Division's top scorer, in the following years, he even descended into alcoholism, though thankfully he sobered up, becoming a hugely loved figure all over again as a TV personality, all quick wit and trenchant opinion delivered with warmth.

Jimmy A too would tread the path to national affection, but his was strewn more with flowers than broken glass. So grounded but broad a life did Jimmy A go on to have that he made manifold marks nationally and locally, in football and outside. One-club men tend to be revered forever – as he was (indeed, still is) in making 627 appearances for Blackpool from 1954 to 1971. (He was, incidentally, booked only once throughout it all, for two fouls in quick succession against Norwich City in an FA Cup tie; some record for a defender.) It could, however, have been tragically different had Sir Matt Busby succeeded in signing him for Manchester United just weeks before the Munich air disaster of 1958, but fortuitously the Blackpool manager Joe Smith refused to let Jimmy go.

Instead, Jimmy developed as an innovative overlapping right-back in the days before wing-backs, making runs with the zeal and cheek of youth in getting beyond the veteran right-winger Stanley Matthews, who was often being double-marked, to receive and cross the ball. It annoyed Smith sometimes, as he liked full-backs who defended, but the fans loved it and it became the pacey, energetic Armfield's trademark.

From playing the game Jimmy became a manager, initially with Bolton Wanderers, then later worked for the Football Association and Professional Footballers' Association as headhunter of England managers and champion of players' causes. He learned, too, the trade of print journalism and TV and radio broadcasting, his mellifluous Lancastrian voice rightly revered when tone and delivery still mattered significantly. This from Daniel Gray, in his 2016 book *Saturday, 3pm: 50 eternal delights of modern football,* is apt: 'His voice is a blessing not only because it helps us float happily to sepia days but also because it conveys his continuing adoration of football… His is a blurring brogue which resonates with depth and honesty, where so much now is sensation and surface.'

Jimmy trained properly in an era before pundits just turned up to the studio or press box thinking their playing career was enough to guarantee them authority. And he opined understatedly but incisively despite a growing preference for shouting and despite perversity of opinion becoming more highly prized by those who hire and commission emptier vessels in search of more youthful listeners.

Away from football, Jimmy played the organ at his parish church, St Peter's. He became a director of the local NHS Hospital Trust and a governor of his old school. He was president of a branch of Age Concern, vice-president of Lancashire Outward Bound and a member of Blackburn Cathedral Council. What else? Well, OBE and CBE, High

Sheriff and then Deputy Lieutenant of Lancashire, all performed with a desire to see young and underprivileged people given help, and a love of life that a serious cancer and subsequent chemotherapy in 2007 unwisely decided to challenge.

I have another hero in the American rock musician Bruce Springsteen, to whom there is devoted a guided tour of his haunts in the small town of Freehold, New Jersey, where he was born and grew up, and venues he first played in the seaside town of Asbury Park. Whenever I visit Blackpool, I feel as if there should be something similar for Jimmy, given that his presence, his spirit, still feels vivid along the now tarnished Golden Mile and in the town's faded backstreets. The town ran through him like its name through a stick of rock bought on the seafront, his physical manifestation still apparent in his statue outside Bloomfield Road and the huge wall mural on the side of a house across the road.

Driving towards Blackpool from Preston after turning off the M6 reminds me of the approach to Atlantic City, another of Bruce's heartland venues, through 'the swamps of Jersey'. As the Jersey Shore nears, big shiny casino hotels loom; from the M55 Blackpool's landmark Tower looms similarly. Often Jim was pictured with it in the background, most notably in that period of injury between the 1962 and 1966 World Cups when the *Evening Gazette* (now the *Blackpool Gazette*) captured him bare-chested running on the South Shore sands. It would be the front-page picture of their loving, rightly award-winning supplement published the day after Jimmy's death on 22 January 2018, aged 82.

Ah, the *Gazette*. Our tour should take in West Street, up near the North Pier, and once the offices of the newspaper where something remarkable happened with Jimmy that would never happen these days – which will be one of the underlying themes of this book, even if modern times carry many echoes of Jim's heyday. From 1959 to 1971 at the height of his fame and football career, Jimmy spent three afternoons a week writing columns for the evening paper, even covering local Wednesday league matches, to gain a grounding in constructing match reports. (Today, in the way of the modern media, where local journalists have little time to mingle with their readership and instead primarily pick up stories from the internet, the *Gazette* is now housed in a business park.)

Perhaps we'll also go to Stanley Park, where Jimmy covered games from an often freezing touchline with no team sheets, just his wits and a pen and notebook. We can see the zoo from there, where the lion ate Albert in that darkly comic Stanley Holloway monologue that began so beautifully: 'There's a famous seaside place called Blackpool/That's noted for fresh air and fun.'

Where to begin the tour? At Tyldesley Road probably, one street back from the Promenade near the Central Pier. It was to a flat above a butcher's shop here that Jimmy's mother Doris brought him from his birthplace at Denton, in Manchester, to escape the bombing in the Second World War. Doris took work at a nearby boarding house and his father, Christopher (Jimmy's middle name), visited at weekends.

After that, rugby union-playing Arnold School, where he excelled even at that sport, right through to the first XV. Football came more informally, learned with a bald tennis ball in the streets and then through more organised Sunday school and youth-club teams, where a Blackpool scout spotted him. He was a natural, though there was no history of the game in his family.

We'll go of course back up by the North Pier, to Talbot Square, where the Town Hall stands. As a 17-year-old junior on Blackpool's books, Jimmy joined the crowds here when the team stood on the steps with the FA Cup after the legendary 4-3 victory over Bolton Wanderers at Wembley in 1953 and what became known as 'The Matthews Final'.

It was to Talbot Square too where Jimmy and his team-mates would later head every Friday afternoon, to the National Provincial Bank to pick up their wages. Now, though the Town Hall is still there, it feels less imposing, the square bisected by tram lines and the surrounding buildings taken prisoner by the modern seaside trade of apartments, bars, kebab shops and 'Blackpool's Premier Lap Dancing Club'. When I last visited, in lashing rain in early August 2022, down The Strand side street gulls picked at bin liners and betting slips littered the pavement. And three things occurred to me.

The first was that, if I concentrated hard as I stood receiving a soaking in Talbot Square and gazed at the Town Hall, I could just imagine Matthews making a speech here, according the plaudits to his team-mates, especially Stan Mortensen, who had scored a hat-trick in the final. The second was that I could also picture an excited teenaged Jimmy Armfield, then playing for the club's junior side, deciding in that moment that he was going to make it as a professional footballer and was going to redouble his efforts to secure an apprenticeship. It would not be long in coming. The third was that – just as I never heard him disparage anyone – never did I hear Jimmy denigrate Blackpool despite its fall into disrepair due to decades-long lack of investment that the 2010s began to address. He remained ever fond of the place and would stand up for it.

Which brings us to St Peter's Church, on the Lytham Road, at the hub of what is now one of Britain's most impoverished, and drug-blighted, areas. The church became Jimmy's 'local' after his marriage to Anne – a remarkable, grounded and intelligent woman who was a nurse by training – and their move to a club house in Rosedale Avenue. At St Peter's, they took Sunday school classes and

Jimmy, having had piano lessons as a boy, agreed to have a go at playing the organ. He did so for more than 50 years in the church that would house his memorable funeral.

For many years, people urged Jimmy to play the mighty, celebrated Wurlitzer organ in the Tower Ballroom but he never felt confident enough. Until his 80th birthday, that was, when a dinner was staged in his honour in the famous hall familiar to generations of dancers and viewers of *Strictly Come Dancing*. For the occasion, Jimmy was finally prevailed upon to play, knowing probably that there might not be another chance, and alongside the expert organist Peter Jebson he essayed – what else? – 'I Do Like to be Beside the Seaside', the organ gradually lowering him beneath the stage to warm applause. There is footage on YouTube that is well worth viewing.

The Tower Ballroom would have to be on any tour itinerary also because in 1959 Blackpool Corporation arranged for Jimmy to be presented there with his Young Player of the Year award by the then England captain Billy Wright, who was about to retire. The place was packed with Saturday-night revellers and, in order to overcome his nerves, Jimmy – then unused to public speaking – needed to draw on all of the calmness that characterised his game and would stand him so well in his life.

From there, we could head back south, to Bairstow Street near Central Pier, and take in the site of the grocery shop that Jimmy's dad took over after joining his family for good after the War, and the flat above it where they lived. From here, Jimmy made deliveries on his bike, even on some Saturday mornings after he made the first team. A few of his friends met him here at lunchtime and together they all walked to Bloomfield Road, where his mates headed for the terraces while Jimmy disappeared through the players' entrance.

We would, naturally, have to take in the rebuilt home of Blackpool FC, a compact all-seater these days rather than the vast-terraced ground of the 1950s that mirrored the club's decline amid the new money and cityscape of the Premier League. There's the stand named after him, of course, and the statue outside, decorated with hundreds of scarves and bouquets of flowers after his death. These days, too, there is that huge mural of him on the side of the house bought by a group of supporters and now called the Armfield Club, a hostelry and social venue for Blackpool fans.

On our way back out of town, before we reach the M55, there are a couple of other places we need to visit. There is his and Anne's final house at South Shore, a few streets back from the Pleasure Beach, in Stony Hill Avenue. No gated community here for Premier League players fearing contact with the real world. It's a pleasant, leafy road and a lovely sizeable semi-detached family home – one for a man, though both local celebrity and well known nationally, at ease among people, his people. The perfect red roof slates tell of the order and neatness of this tidy residential road. At the back of the house is the conservatory Jimmy loved sitting in to admire his manicured lawn that was bordered by his prized geraniums and roses.

From Stony Hill Avenue, it is some 500 metres to the small Blackpool Airport and, adjacent, the Squires Gate training ground of Blackpool FC where our tour could even start but, if not, should certainly finish. Having been effectively sacked as manager by Leeds United in 1978, in the subsequent months and years Jimmy would head to the training ground of his playing days, this time to offer his help – taken up by club managers – as an unpaid coach. He was not too proud nor his ego so large that he couldn't muck in. He needed something active to do in the game after being hurt by his Elland Road departure – somewhere familiar and comforting.

Indeed, the experience meant that, despite contemplating the odd job opportunity, he never again subjected himself to football management, a profession that had been revealed to him first hand as brutal and unforgiving, even if he thought he was good at it and had a suitable temperament, mixing carrot and stick. The sheer ruthlessness of it was certainly seen in Brian Clough's dismissal at Leeds as successor to the revered Don Revie, though it was not Jimmy's initial experience in 1974/75 after being appointed, in turn, as Clough's successor. That season would be one of the most remarkable in English football during an astonishingly eventful and earthy time for the game.

2

BACK IN the 17th century, the philosopher Thomas Hobbes wrote that life was 'nasty, brutish and short'. In 1970's England, football was nasty, British and sport.

There has been handed down an idyllic vision of the English game in the 1960s, with footage of the 1966 World Cup win seeming to show a cheery, chummy set of spectators revelling in its sheer exuberance, all rosettes and rattles making a racket. By the end of the decade, however, tribalism was beginning to prevail, perhaps stoked by an arrogance that the English were now officially the world's best – an impression that lingered through to the 1970s, perhaps never to disappear in many supporters. Hooliganism duly blighted the decade, a police force struggling to suppress it all at a time when there was no technology to help them, such as CCTV cameras in and around grounds. Ambushes and fights would take place on trains and in backstreets. Brazenly, away fans tried to 'take' home ends. I know because I was there, running its gauntlet. Or, more accurately, trying to dodge it.

It is worth recalling the backdrop of the times, both socially and politically. These were strange, remarkable days, as raw as the game itself, even though much of its precariousness and danger passed me by, imbued as I was with the nonchalance of youth. In 1973, I had started at London University – my lovely Bedford College in the middle of Regent's Park offering a haven from what in hindsight seems like chaos but at the time felt enervating – amid a backdrop of the IRA bombing campaign in London. Inflation was running at 8 per cent, with wage rises limited to 7 per cent in a bid to curb that inflation.

Feeling out of my depth academically and somewhat lost in the big city after an upbringing in a small backwater town, I soon sought refuge in watching football and going to see the huge rock bands of the time – Led Zeppelin, Yes, Deep

Purple. It seems astonishing now but as a student I could afford it, also going to Arsenal, Chelsea and other matches. We didn't then realise how fortunate we were that local authorities paid fees and even maintenance grants. That was just how it was. I for one certainly took it for granted.

By January 1974, as I began my second term, the country was in an energy crisis that meant a three-day working week and the first recession since the War. To me – still a kid whose political awareness was growing – it all seemed a bit of an adventure, especially when First Division matches were played on midweek afternoons to avert the need for floodlights. I remember seeing Chelsea play Burnley in front of a crowd of around 8,000.

There was a worry that the country might lurch to the right in such divisive times, with striking workers seeking pay rises to ease the pain of inflation. They were portrayed by the right as wreckers of society. Meanwhile, Enoch Powell stirred racial issues with his notorious, odious 'rivers of blood' speech. The Conservative Prime Minister Edward Heath called an election for the February seeking a mandate to sort out the strikers.

I headed back to Dorset to vote for the first time. A hung parliament resulted and Heath tried, and failed, to enter a coalition with the Liberals. Labour instead, under Harold Wilson, formed a minority government that limped on until October, when Wilson called another election. This time, there was a majority for him and his party.

In between, history records some remarkable events. The IRA campaign intensified with the appalling Guildford and Birmingham pub bombings. From my college hall of residence near Baker Street, I would hear other (smaller but still loud) explosions in Central London. It was also the year that Lord Lucan disappeared after the murder of a nanny at his London home. On a lighter note, ABBA won the Eurovision Song Contest in Brighton (interval act: The Wombles) with the career-launchpad song 'Waterloo'.

Spring and summer also saw momentous times in football. Manchester United were relegated from the First Division, their great striker Denis Law, who had moved to Manchester City (yes, unthinkable again now), confirming their fall with an almost apologetic backheel home in the penultimate match of the season. And, in a development that stunned the football world, the most successful manager in English football history, the revered and legendary Bill Shankly, announced his retirement from Liverpool, to be succeeded by Bob Paisley.

England football and the nation, though, had another managerial manoeuvre of its own to concern it.

The previous October, to the country's utter amazement and disgust, England could only draw 1-1 with Poland at Wembley and failed to qualify for the following summer's World Cup finals in West Germany. There was disbelief, given 1966 and the reaching of the 1970 quarter-finals in Mexico, where the Germans had come from 2-0 down to win 3-2 in a notable act of revenge for the 4-2 at Wembley. After Poland, Sir Alf Ramsey paid the price with his job, though it took the FA six months to see the deed through, possibly because they were waiting for their next man to finish what was a championship-winning season.

As Ramsey's successor, Don Revie was really the only logical choice. He had been manager of Leeds United since 1960 and the end of his playing days with the club. He had lifted them from Second Division obscurity to top-flight pre-eminence in the late 1960s and early 1970s, winning five trophies: the League Cup in 1968, the Inter-Cities Fairs Cup (an early version of the UEFA Cup) in 1971, the FA Cup in 1972 and the First Division title in both 1969, and 1974, the year the FA secured his services. Often Leeds' football was admirably fluent but it was accompanied by their reputation as exponents of the dark arts at a time when physicality was more leniently treated. Revie's teams, often accorded the soubriquet 'Dirty Leeds', were regularly decried as cynical, their talent only grudgingly acknowledged. Norman 'Bites Yer Legs' Hunter and the fiery, feisty Billy Bremner were the teak-tough emblems, the collective ethic built on fierce loyalty to manager, each other and the cause. The conceding of a goal was seen as personal. The opposition were to be punished severely for such effrontery.

It was why there were some reservations about the FA's appointment of Revie to the England job, the game's pinnacle then for a manager. They were, after all, supposedly the guardians of the game and its integrity on and off the pitch. Certainly

Revie's successor at Leeds, Brian Clough, felt little reverence towards him. Indeed, Clough – a much-sought-after TV pundit because of his outspoken views – had called for Leeds to be relegated because of their disciplinary record. Years later, the film of David Peace's 'faction' novel *The Damned United*, in which Michael Sheen was perfect as Clough, would dramatise the famous speech of him telling the Leeds players on his first day in the job to consign their medals to the dustbin because they had all been won by cheating. It was little surprise, therefore, that those players would be publicly sceptical and privately antagonistic towards him following his appointment on 24 July to succeed the paternal Revie.

The then Leeds United reporter for the *Yorkshire Evening Post*, Don Warters, who spent 29 years in the post before becoming a press officer for the club, remembers the times well.

'It was not a happy time for me personally,' he told me. 'I'd been on holiday when Brian Clough took over, and when I got back the *Daily Mail* had run a story saying that several players were refusing to sign new contracts and I had to ask him about it. I introduced myself to him and walked through the car park with him and asked the question. He said, "It's all a load of balls. And if you ask me that question again, I'll kick you over the fucking stand." I never got on with him at all.'

After the inauspicious beginning off the field came one to shock on it. Actually, there was an equal amount of *Schadenfreude* at the travails of a club a bit too flash for the liking of most people outside Elland Road, flashness that included the Admiral kit, players' names on the back of tracksuits, sock tags, and the change of club badge from peacock to what looked like the smiley logo that was doing the rounds at the time.

First there was a brutal FA Charity Shield at Wembley against Liverpool that saw Johnny Giles punch Kevin Keegan, who in turn was sent off along with Bremner after a separate incident. Liverpool won 6-5 on penalties. Then, come the opening day of the season, Leeds lost 3-0 to Stoke City (I recall being on a camping holiday in France and cajoling the commentary out of a radio and hearing it, astonished). Outright mutiny would ensue and the Leeds board, seeing the players as the greater asset, ended Clough's tenure on 12 September after just 44 days as the champions sat 19th in the table after only one win in six games. Clough departed with a cheque for £98,000, a huge sum at the time.

The following night he appeared in studio 2 at Yorkshire TV for their evening news programme *Calendar,* being interviewed alongside Revie by the presenter Austin Mitchell, who went on to become an MP, in a coup of journalism hastily arranged by the news editor John Wilford. It was compulsive and confrontational viewing, the two men's contempt for each other uncontainable. Yet another it-wouldn't-happen-now moment, probably even for a sizeable fee, as the £5,000 each of the two men received was.

Enter, stage right, our hero: Gentleman Jim, as he was already known. After his retirement from playing three years earlier at the age of 35, Jimmy could have gone into journalism there and then, knowing the ropes from his experiences with the *Evening Gazette.* However, a stint as player-manager of an England squad making an 11-game goodwill tour of Tahiti, New Zealand and the Far East in the summer of 1969 (add that to the 'unthinkable now' list) had given him a taste for management beyond a simple desire to stay in the game. Or, more accurately in the case of many professionals, beyond a fear of letting it go at a time when the most popular post-playing options were still running a pub or opening a sports shop.

He'd hoped that Blackpool might have recruited him to the coaching staff but he knew the ways of football: that any manager in situ would be looking over his shoulder at a club legend easily appointed as his replacement should the board be considering a sacking. (At that time, it was Bob Stokoe, who famously went on to lead then Second Division Sunderland to an FA Cup win over Revie's Leeds in 1973.)

Blackburn Rovers approached Jimmy but he opted for Bolton Wanderers, newly relegated to the Third Division, because he felt that the chairman Jack Banks was a man he could work with. It was a decision Jimmy never regretted, though years later, his son John told me, there was something that did make him wistful.

'He thought when he looked back that he could have played another two or three years. He had an offer from Arsenal, from Don Howe, who was coaching there, to go there after they won the Double because they wanted a bit of experience at right-back but he didn't want to go to London. When he got the Bolton job, he did think about playing in the centre of midfield. But he was told he would be arthritic by the age of 40. He said later that it wouldn't have mattered because he was arthritic at 40 anyway.'

After a patchy start in his first season, in the second he won them the division and promotion. It brought him to the attention of Everton in April 1973, the board looking for a successor to the retiring Harry Catterick, but Jimmy felt he was not ready. Some 18 months later, when Leeds came in, he was.

'I think when the Liverpool job came up, he did think he might have a chance at that,' John said. 'He used to go into the boot room with Shankly and he was well liked there.' The in-house appointment of Paisley would come to prove inspired, though, as 20 trophies including six titles and three European Cups attested.

The toxic atmosphere around Leeds all seemed a very unappealing environment for a placid man like Jimmy Armfield. Especially given that everyone knew this was an ageing team and squad in need of rebuilding over the next year or two. Perhaps that was why Revie decamped, even though there was the alluring prospect of a campaign in the European Cup.

In actual fact, Jimmy was the perfect man and the Leeds board knew it after the ill-starred Clough era, and on the principle that a new manager is often required to be the antidote to the previous one. Where Clough was abrasive, Jimmy would be accommodating. Also, for Armfield the budding manager, it was a job that could not be turned down, regrets rampant if he hadn't taken it.

'They'd experienced the explosive stuff and I've no doubt they saw Jimmy as a steadying influence,' said Don Warters, whose first encounter with Jim could not have been much more different than his debut dealing with Clough. 'I remember when I first met him, at the entrance to the main stand, I was taken by how relaxed he looked. He was very knowledgeable and highly rated by the FA, even if he wasn't that experienced.'

Jimmy probably also had the Revie stamp of approval. In his autobiography, Jim tells of being invited to London by Revie just before Clough's sacking to discuss a job with the FA as the England Under-23 manager. In the end, no offer materialised and Jimmy came to believe that Revie was almost interviewing him for the Leeds job, reporting back to players and board about his suitability, including his healing powers.

I remember following it all via the newspapers strewn about the college union that autumn of 1974 as a football-hungry teen still, though I was, it has to be admitted, more interested in the fortunes of Weymouth back then. The more so when, as a Southern League club, they held the old Division Three leaders Peterborough to a goalless draw at London Road in the first round of the FA Cup. The replay was drawn 3-3 after extra time at our old Recreation Ground before losing the second replay 3-0 at Peterborough. I must have spent a week's grant going to all three games.

Anyway, Jimmy himself seemed to have no concerns about the job being, in the time-honoured phrase, a poisoned chalice, even if when he arrived on 4 October, two weeks past his 39th birthday, Leeds had lost two more of their three games in the period after Clough's departure. Those came under the caretaker management of Maurice Lindley, a sort of coach-cum-general manager of the team and a well-liked figure around the club. Jim also believed that this team – one that most critics believed was past its best – had one last hurrah in it.

'Dad also got on well with Cloughie,' said John Armfield. 'I'm sure they would have talked about it as well. Dad would have had confidence in himself. He never took a risk.'

Not that some others had total belief in him. 'He was an unassuming man,' said Warters. 'He was relaxed and quietly spoken. My first thought was, "How's he going to do this difficult job?" He just didn't look management material on the outside.'

Some of the players wondered too. Years later, one of Clough's signings, Duncan McKenzie, would say: 'Jimmy was like the nice neighbour that everyone wants next door.'

Jim also came without baggage and had one huge thing in his favour: he was not Brian Clough. And mild-mannered as he was, he soon proved his shrewdness in an evolving plan that saw McKenzie thrust into centre stage after being marginalised in the squad along with other distrusted Clough signings in John O'Hare and John McGovern.

'I needed to get rid of the sour feeling, the sour taste,' Jimmy said some 35 years later. 'I wanted to get the team back on its feet and I thought we needed a bonding exercise.' Over a discussion with a Leeds fan – a well-connected one – he came up with an idea that might just fit the bill.

3

BARNEY COLEHAN was born in the village of Calverley, about ten miles north of Leeds, and was a fan of the club, a regular in the lounges at Elland Road. He also happened to be a big noise in the BBC, producer of two of their biggest TV shows of the 1970s – *It's a Knockout*, a knockabout game show with myriad, mad physical challenges in crazy costumes played between rival towns at leisure centres and playing fields, and *The Good Old Days*, a singalong and dance bill based on the Victorian music halls and filmed at the City Varieties Theatre in Leeds, which Colehan ran.

On our televisions for 30 years, the latter will be remembered by those of us of a certain age who were subjected to dull three-channel nights when school or college work suddenly seemed appealing.

One day in early autumn not long after becoming Leeds manager, Jimmy invited Colehan – who had produced an *It's a Knockout* special ahead of Leeds' FA Cup Final win over Arsenal in 1972 – into his office at Elland Road to discuss the annual Christmas knees-up for the players, along with the day-after traditional party for their wives and children. Jim thought he might bring a bit of showbiz pizzazz to proceedings.

They first discussed a fancy-dress party at the stadium, behind closed doors. But 'one thing led to another', as Jimmy wrote in his autobiography, and he suggested that he might himself write a pantomime for the players. Colehan immediately grew excited, said that they could put it on at the City Varieties and he could 'make a few bob out of it'. Some could go to charity and the rest to Paul Reaney's testimonial fund, they agreed.

Jimmy had decided not to move the family to Leeds, though they did look at a house near Ilkley early on in his time at the club. He did not wish to uproot John, then 11, and 13-year-old Duncan (named after Jim's great friend in the England Under-21 side, Duncan Edwards of Manchester

United, who died tragically in the 1958 Munich air disaster) from Arnold School, where Jimmy had been a pupil. Back home in Blackpool in the evenings, he began to write a script, by his own admission stealing jokes from various sources.

'I remember him writing,' said John. 'He wrote lots of things, including a song. He'd light his pipe. Don Howe, who he got in at Leeds later as a coach to help with the defence, used to say that you knew he was thinking hard when he lit his pipe. He always had time for us, and for Mother, but when he did that, you knew you weren't going to get much out of him.'

(That pipe… Less physically damaging than the all-pervasive cigarettes at the time – you could even smoke on the London Underground – the briar had been made famous by Harold Wilson. He cannily used a draw on it during interviews, as permitted on TV, to buy himself time to find the right answer. Perhaps Jimmy got his cue from the Prime Minister.)

Jim had chosen the tried-and-trusted story of Cinderella for his panto and after a couple of weeks had enough to show Colehan. He asked him to come in to the office and outlined the plan and the script, wanting also to discuss costumes. Colehan apparently was astonished that Jimmy had been serious and had made such progress. He was immediately and enthusiastically on board.

Now Jimmy went to the players with the idea. And here, it has to be said, memories can diverge, including his own. In his autobiography, he recalled that they 'entered into it with relish'. When interviewed about the episode for *FourFourTwo* magazine in 2009, however, he said: 'They all looked at me like I had gone mad.'

Norman Hunter later admitted to being especially sceptical, thinking it 'stupid' and wondering just who would buy tickets for it. Duncan McKenzie thought it smart, a way of bonding the players. As it happened, Jimmy was shrewder even than that. As Hunter noted in the *FourFourTwo* article, the players were already bonded – but this was a good way of integrating McKenzie into the group and also Jimmy establishing himself with them. 'You have to remember, he was then only four or five years older than a lot of them,' said John Armfield. But they began chewing it over, noting that a lot of the proceeds would be going to charity and the Reaney testimonial fund.

'I think we were a bit surprised rather than against it,' Reaney told me. 'We were used to big Christmas parties, where we'd have games for the kids and the wives would sing, but this was a bit different. When they thought about it, people could see what he was trying to do. In those days, you needed your testimonial and there were a lot of us coming up to ten years' service to the club. I was OK with it, and I think others came to see it could be good as well.' Among them was Hunter, the following year's recipient of a testimonial.

By now, results were improving. In the run-up to Christmas, Leeds won five and drew one of their eight First Division games. In the period between Clough and Armfield, under the caretaker-management of Maurice Lindley, they had beaten FC Zurich 5-3 on aggregate in the first round of the European Cup. In the second round, in late October and early November under Jimmy, they disposed of the Hungarians Újpest Dózsa 5-1 over the two legs. (Gates from those days are always surprising, from today's perspective: there were only 28,091 at Elland

Road for the 3-0 win in the second leg.) That took them through to the quarter-finals. Against that, shockingly for their fans and to show they were not entirely out of the woods, they went out of the League Cup, 3-0 at Chester.

By and large, however, casting and rehearsals for the panto – twice a week after training – were conducted against a more settled backdrop and in a more relaxed environment. A date was set for the week before Christmas and such were ticket sales, the theatre selling out in an hour, that another date was hastily added. McKenzie was assigned the role of Cinderella and Reaney that of Prince Charming. In an inspired piece of casting, the diminutive firebrand Bremner was to be Buttons. The imposing Gordon McQueen, who later joined Manchester United, became the Good Fairy McQueen.

In an idea probably inspired by the host's role of Leonard Sachs in *The Good Old Days,* Jimmy was to be the narrator, standing at the side of the stage in top hat and red morning coat, armed with a copy of the script, typed up by his secretary Maureen. It meant that he would be ready for the – many – occasions on which the players forgot their lines.

And it would always provoke a laugh, he knew. Mistakes were going to be part of the fun. More seriously, it meant that he also had control of events and a position of authority. His script contained plenty of the traditional old line 'He's behind you' – and Jimmy was. He was transmitting a message to them that he had their backs.

On the day the script was first presented to the players, there was trepidation amongst them. Then relief. 'Because you could see it would work,' said McKenzie. At his/her entrance, Jimmy announced, 'Here comes Cinders, straight from the Forest.' 'It ended up getting a big laugh,' McKenzie remembered.

'There was a lot of laughter at the first rehearsal,' Jimmy told *FourFourTwo* in 2009. 'I'd written a lot of corny jokes but they were jokes that related to the players. There were a few jokes about a pantomime off the pitch and a pantomime on it but they really got down to it.' The players did indeed respond. The doubting Hunter said: 'We just chucked ourselves into it.'

Don Warters remembers the same with Billy Bremner. 'I used to write a weekly column for him and he mentioned it all to me. He took it in, entered into the spirit of it. I think they all did.'

Panto rehearsals and any sense of fun they engendered were never going to win matches – it needed footballing talent and performances to achieve that – but there was no doubt that the mood of the club was undergoing an improvement. Come opening night, there was an air of excitement about everyone as Jimmy delivered one of the most unusual managerial dressing-room team talks in history.

'Billy was there in his little cap and tails, the Good Fairy McQueen was there in her tutu,' Jimmy said in his autobiography. 'I told them that the greatest managers in the world had never given a talk like this to players who looked like they did. Then I said, "Does anyone need a drink?" I'd read that some theatre people needed a drink. It was brandy, I think, and a few of them had a nip for nerves. I was one of the few who had a nip.'

'Looking back,' John Armfield remembered, 'they were all half-cut.'

Reaney passed. 'I'm teetotal,' he told me. 'We had lots of characters who could carry it off, but as

Prince Charming I had some responsibility. Jimmy was a clever man in how he used to talk to people. He told me when he arrived that I was the best right-back in the country and I could get back into the England side. And he told me I was going to be the best Prince Charming.'

As well as alcohol, there were cigarettes. When the curtain parted, a huge roar went up in the theatre, McKenzie recollecting that people were sitting in the aisles and standing at the back, somehow having escaped the ushers. 'You couldn't do it now, with health and safety,' McKenzie noted 35 years later. But apparently you could lift your dress, as he did at one point in an ad-lib departure from the script, take a cigarette from his stocking top and light up, sharing the tab with the notoriously heavy smoker Bremner, or rather Buttons. 'The crowd loved that,' said Jimmy in *Right Back to the Beginning.*

The action began with Cinders working away in the kitchen and narrator Jimmy setting the scene. He wondered where Buttons was – twice, to get the audience immediately involved. At the third time of asking, Bremner appeared at the back of the theatre. Said Jimmy: 'Billy came skipping down the centre aisle with his brass buttons and his pill box hat, throwing out sweets to the kids. He was a natural, Billy. He should have been on the stage.' Bremner then spent a couple of minutes with disabled children at the front before depositing the jar of sweets at the side of the stage, demanding the audience tell him if anyone tried to steal them. He may have been a softie at heart – 'He loved kids and he loved the people,' said Norman Hunter – but nobody was going to take anything off Leeds.

And he did love kids. Duncan and John Armfield recall him coming down to where the players' families were sitting and leading the children up on stage.

'I didn't like it much but I went up with Duncan,' said John. 'We had to sing "Rudolf the Red Nosed Reindeer". We were all right with the first verse but then we had to sing the second and nobody knew it.'

'But then, there were a lot of lines being fluffed,' added Duncan. 'I did think it was good, though.'

Indeed, even when it didn't go smoothly, it went well. Terry Yorath was one of the Ugly Sisters and his big moment had him singing a song, 'Sonny Boy', with Bremner sat on his knee. The very vision of it speaks comedy, which increased with Yorath beginning the song several times and having to start again because his opening was so bad. After the pianist had given him the key several times, they all gave up and Yorath sang it out of tune anyway.

'The Welsh are supposed to be able to sing but Terry proved there's an exception to every rule,' Jimmy said in his autobiography.

The running time of the script was 60 minutes but such was the audience reaction – the cheering and clapping, along with the players' growing into their parts and building them up and milking their lines – that it stretched to an appropriate 90 minutes. The applause at the end was loud and long.

'It was packed,' John Armfield recalled. 'I remember all the girls screaming at Frank Gray, Joe Jordan, Gordon McQueen. We were brought up in football, and the Blackpool players' names would roll off our tongues, but they wouldn't roll off anyone's tongues outside the town. These were internationals and I think we were in awe.'

'We got a lot of appreciation,' said Reaney. 'The crowd was brilliant and it all went very well.' And the proceeds certainly helped his testimonial fund. 'I did OK,' he said, with a match against Newcastle United also helping.

Warters was less impressed, but 'It was quite a success,' he admitted. 'It was just players being silly really but the fans lapped it up. I wrote three pantos myself for my local church. Mine were better.'

Afterwards, Duncan and John stayed with Anne and Jimmy in Leeds for a few days, as they often did in the school holidays, at the Dragonara or Queen's hotels. They took in the kids' annual party at the club, Maurice Lindley as Father Christmas.

'The players would hand out presents to us,' said John. 'At Blackpool, you'd get a cracker and a handshake. They were handing out all sorts at Leeds. I remember Duncan getting a cassette player and me being very jealous.'

'It was brilliant,' said Duncan. 'I had that for a few years.'

CHAPTER 3

Impresario Colehan, who died in 1991, was left lamenting that he might have had an even bigger Christmas present. He could, he said, have sold out a one-month run. Instead, he had to settle for a one-night-only reprise in November 1975. This time, though, a funny thing happened on the way to the theatre.

During a game at Derby at the beginning of that month, Hunter had been sent off after a punch-up with Francis Lee as a result of bad blood lingering due to Leeds players believing that Lee had dived for a penalty. A melee ensued, with both players being dismissed and ending up before an FA disciplinary panel.

TV footage had failed to capture some of the original incident but had caught Lee flailing at Hunter and connecting well enough to knock him over. Lee was fined £250 and given a four-match ban. Hunter, his role in it mostly missed, got away with no further punishment beyond the red card. Thus it was a lucky-feeling Hunter who climbed into Jimmy Armfield's car after the hearing to head north for the reprise performance of *Cinderella*, this time taking the part of Prince Charming as the season's beneficiary of a testimonial. There was to be no missing this role.

When Hunter made his entrance, Jimmy introduced him with: 'Here's Baron Diver, back from London.' He then borrowed Bruce Forsyth's voice and catchphrase from *The Generation Game*, the hit Saturday-evening show of the time, declaring 'Didn't we do well?' to a rapturous reception from the easiest crowd any performer could want.

From being the player with the most reservations about the whole venture – someone wondering who would possibly want to buy a ticket for it – Hunter ended up fully on board and loved the experience. And this time, the production was much slicker for the experience of the first.

'I had to say, "Whoever's foot this slipper fits will be my Queen,"' Hunter said some years later. 'I might have got it wrong in rehearsal but on the night your professionalism came out. Nobody wanted to make the first mistake. We were word-perfect almost. It was the excitement. And I'm not like that myself but I got the feeling that some of the lads quite enjoyed the dressing-up.'

Both events had achieved what Jimmy had set out to do: to raise the spirits of a club that had known only sourness and suspicion for many months. It would take a man like him – not that there were many such men – to achieve it, making the Leeds chairman Manny Cussins and the club's board look like clever operators after the pillorying they had received from players, fans and press over the appointment of Clough. They would not deserve to be regarded so well in their dealings with Jimmy as time unfolded.

The pantomime also serves the purpose of distilling the essence of Jimmy. Benign and affable, yes, but shrewd and strategic too. All carried off with aplomb and with none resenting him. He took people with him by engaging them rather than bullying them.

'Jimmy knew from the start that one of his jobs was to continue the job that Cloughie had started and to break up that great team,' said McKenzie. 'But with things like the panto, he was able to do it in a nice way, a gentlemanly way. Not shock tactics like Cloughie.'

I asked Duncan and John Armfield if they were ever embarrassed by the whole pantomime episode, in the way that sons are by the daft-looking actions of their fathers – the dad-dancing syndrome. They pretty much chorused, 'Not at all.'

'He had utter confidence in his ability to do things,' Duncan replied.

'It was sickening,' said John, a smile on his face. 'He could do anything. We'd go on holiday abroad and there would be a tennis tournament with some Germans who looked a bit good. All the English would be saying, "Go on Jim. Take them on." And he would. And he'd beat them. That was Dad.'

'It was the same with the annual snooker competition at the local club,' added Duncan. 'He might not have played for months but he'd still win it.'

I asked them if they ever felt under pressure, given that their father was such a high-achiever with a big public profile.

'Never,' said Duncan. 'He never made me feel that way.'

John felt a little differently, mainly because he had been a keen footballer during his teens and, as a goalkeeper, was taken on by Manchester United, for whom he played in the FA Youth Cup.

'I don't think it was easy,' he said. 'I didn't ever want to let him down. It's easy if your dad's playing in the Fourth Division but when he's captain of England, it's different. They used to call me SOJ – Son Of Jim.' He had enjoyed, though, coming out of the ground with his dad after a Youth Cup tie against Derby County and being asked for his autograph by a youngster, with Jimmy being ignored.

(John would also tell me how he was offered a place at university and asked his father what he should do: try and win a professional contract in the game or take up the place? Jimmy advised him, with candour and John's best interests at heart, to go to university. Never has he regretted it, having enjoyed a career in non-league football alongside teaching.)

As well as Jim's many victories, naturally there were losses, too, including the biggest one of his life, coming in between those two pantomimes of December 1974 and November 1975. Indeed, it would be a seismic event in the history of Leeds United, an episode so controversial – even criminal, he felt – that it left Jimmy the angriest his sons had ever seen him. A season that had begun so sourly but been rescued by Jimmy would end with probably the saddest night of his footballing life.

Indeed, it also became a pivotal moment in the club's history. Jimmy said years later that he'd have liked to make the pantomime an annual event, but it became impossible with the changes in personnel needed. He would get one last tune out of the group he had inherited but – in a nod to another huge TV show that Barney Colehan was involved in during its early days – he could not quite make them *Top of the Pops*.

4

MY MOBILE rang. It was April 2012 and Jimmy was on the other end. 'Eh, that Chelsea result last night... Reminded me of Leeds. There were so many similarities between us then and Chelsea now.'

Indeed there were. Chelsea had just drawn 2-2 in Barcelona to go through 3-2 on aggregate to the Champions League Final, under a manager in Roberto Di Matteo who had not long taken over after an unhappy episode involving a young manager with a big reputation. André Villas-Boas had lasted longer than Brian Clough – some eight months in total – but a group of senior players had turned on him after questioning his tactics and selections.

We should do a piece about it, Jimmy said. And so we did. I was grateful to him. I was coming to the end of my career writing for newspapers, freelancing now, and the fee from the subsequent article with him was most welcome.

Come the early spring of 1975, Jimmy had turned both mood and results at Elland Road. They had lost the first game after the panto, 3-0 to Newcastle United, to fuel a few press comments mixing jokes with criticism that they had spent too much time rehearsing and not training, and were not focused on the job in hand – that of climbing away from a position too close to the foot of the table for comfort. From then until March, however, more probably buoyed by the improved atmosphere that the manager had created, they went unbeaten for ten games, winning six and drawing four. They also had a good FA Cup run, reaching the quarter-finals before losing in a THIRD replay (another it-can't-happen-now event) to a high quality Ipswich Town side managed by Bobby Robson.

Alongside all that, upon the resumption of the European Cup in the March, Leeds saw off the Belgian club Anderlecht over two legs in the quarter-final, and impressively: by 3-0 and 1-0. It took them to an April semi-final against Barcelona, where Johan Cruyff was then in his pomp, having led his national team less than a year earlier to a World Cup Final against West Germany in which the Netherlands showed themselves to be probably the best team never to win the trophy.

An Allan Clarke goal gave Leeds a 2-1 home win in front of a crowd of 50,393 at Elland Road but many thought that Leeds would succumb in the Camp Nou in front of more than double that number. Peter Lorimer scored early and, though Gordon McQueen was sent off, Leeds held on for a 1-1 draw and a 3-2 aggregate win.

'I remember the physio Bob English having to go on to attend to a player with eight minutes to go,' John Armfield said. 'What with him dropping towels, pretending to the referee that his heart was giving him trouble, it must have taken him eight and a half minutes to get on and off. Dad always said it was the best performance ever by a physio.'

Jimmy may have been the antidote to old days and ways at Leeds but all football people will tell you that there are times – none bigger than this – when a job just has to be done in whatever way was needed. Finally the whistle blew and Leeds were through to a final against Bayern Munich in Paris. Jimmy had been right: this team did have a last hurrah in them.

'We had the experience within the team to hold on,' Jimmy told me that April day in 2012. 'Paul Madeley was a Rolls-Royce alongside Norman Hunter at the back. It was a performance of dogged determination and no little skill.'

And, Paul Reaney later told me: 'The thing about Jimmy was that he was a good listener. Don Revie had taught us a lot and we were an experienced side. He knew we had a lot of knowledge ourselves and he knew not to interfere sometimes. I remember how he lit his pipe and listened.'

That Jimmy had phoned me to talk about Chelsea – who had John Terry sent off in the second leg and were facing Lionel Messi at his magnificent best in an echo of McQueen and Cruyff – was so typical of the man. He was just enthused by the game, still in love with it at the age of 76, no matter the way it had treated him sometimes. He had woken up that morning, had a thought and wanted to talk about football and his experiences.

'Both started the season under new management, full of hope and with a lot of expectation,' Jimmy continued about the similarities between Chelsea and Leeds. And both André Villas-Boas and Clough inherited teams created by others. The difference was Clough only had 44 days and Chelsea were nearer the top of the table while Leeds were looking towards the bottom.

'That was all I needed to say in my first team talk: what are such a good group of players doing near the bottom of the First Division? They responded to that.'

Jimmy reminded me that he had turned down the job at Everton a year before joining Leeds as he had not felt ready to take on a big club at that time. 'I wonder if the same was true of Villas-Boas, especially coming from another country,' he said, going on to offer real insights into his first year at Leeds. 'You have to man-manage yourself as well, especially with strong characters around the place. I did hear him talk about moving older players on and I thought "that's fatal". A good card player keeps his cards close to his chest. Some people said

I was indecisive but I knew where I was going. I just didn't make things public.

'The players were entrenched in Don Revie's ways but that was quite right – he had done a lot for their careers. I went along with them because the truth was they knew more about European football than I did. That's part of man-management.'

There was one other huge similarity for Chelsea and Leeds: Bayern would also be the London club's final opponents. However, sadly for Jimmy, and Leeds, there was to be one last big difference. While Chelsea overcame enormous odds to prevail over Bayern in their own stadium, on penalties, Leeds were beaten 2-0 against a backdrop of crowd trouble in the Parc des Princes. They were denied a penalty when the French referee Michel Kitabdjian strangely failed to deem a Franz Beckenbauer challenge on Allan Clarke a foul, then ruled out a volleyed Peter Lorimer goal with the score at 0-0, deeming that Billy Bremner was in an offside position – though only Beckenbauer, belatedly, had appealed.

'Beckenbauer,' Don Warters told me, 'was talking to the referee the whole game, trying to influence him.'

'We were the better side,' Jimmy insisted. 'We had a goal disallowed and a blatant penalty turned down but it was overlooked due to the problems with supporters and then Leeds being banned from Europe for four years.'

This was Jimmy at his most diplomatic, time having healed much. In fact, he was fuming on the night, as were Leeds. The refereeing decisions left him convinced something was amiss. Duncan and John were up in the stands, with Anne.

'It was terrible,' Duncan recalled. 'It was the worst match I have ever been to. I was convinced something wasn't right. I remember Dad saying later that he turned to Bob English during the game and said they needed this to be 0-0, to get a different referee for a replay, because they weren't going to be allowed to win. I've never seen Dad as angry as he was afterwards. He wanted to throw his medal away but Mum wouldn't let him.'

'At the hotel afterwards it was like a wake,' John added. 'Most of these players knew it was their last chance.'

In his autobiography, Jimmy told of how a lot of Leeds fans were vilified for being drunk, but he cited mitigation in the fact that the stadium, unbeknown to arriving spectators, was 'dry' and their duty-free alcohol purchases were being confiscated at the turnstiles. It prompted many to drink them there and then. The disturbances, which included some angry fans ripping out and hurling seats, led to Leeds being banned from Europe for four seasons but Jimmy was not going to take that lying down.

'He did very well, both that season and after the final,' said Don Warters. 'He worked really hard and spent hours formulating an appeal.'

Jimmy told me in 2012: 'I found out a few things were not right with the organisation of the match and I managed to get the ban reduced to two years when people said I had no chance.' In fact, Leeds directors told him to drop the matter but he refused to. So eloquently did he plead the club's case – even threatening to go public with his doubts about the referee's probity – that UEFA were persuaded.

There was no bitterness in Jimmy's voice as he spoke. That ability to accept life's slings and arrows and to view them dispassionately years later was part of his admirable, enviable temperament. That day on the phone, he was also enthused by the prospect of presenting the FA Cup to the winners of the Chelsea v Liverpool final at Wembley the following week, having been chosen by the Football Association for the honour.

'I could never have envisaged it in the years after the War,' he said. 'First playing at Wembley then leading the England team out... Now I get to present the FA Cup as well. It's every boy's dream.'

Players and people in the game say that all the time, about something being a dream. I think some players may even be taught it in media training sessions. With Jimmy, still a boyishness about him, you knew at that moment that he meant it.

Actually, there did come a time when his enthusiasm and love of the game was sorely tested by slings and arrows. And it came at Leeds, with more than an element of the outrageous about his fortune. After the European Cup Final came the task that Jimmy knew needed addressing – the course of action that Brian Clough and the Leeds board of directors had known needed to be taken.

'Don Revie had always said that the hardest job was going to be dismantling the side,' said Warters. Perhaps, after all, there was a sentimentality within Revie (who would quit the England job to take a lucrative appointment in the United Arab Emirates as England were on the verge of failing to qualify for the 1978 World Cup), albeit a hidden one. Such a sentimentality might have meant he did not want to perform the surgery at Leeds on players he loved like a father and thus he accepted readily the England post.

'The old guard started to disappear,' Norman Hunter said. 'I went to Bristol City, Billy went to Hull, Gilesy went to West Brom. It was the end of an era and we didn't feel bitter towards Jimmy for that, even though I think a few of us could have carried on for longer.'

The break-up had begun before Paris, with Jim allowing John McGovern and John O'Hare to rejoin Clough, who by then had taken over at Nottingham Forest, and it soon gathered pace. In all, 13 players departed over the next three years, ten of them internationals. In came some major signings, not least as his first-team coach Don

Howe, an old England team-mate and revered strategist. The player who sprinkled stardust and gave the team a new creativity was the mercurial Tony Currie, from Sheffield United, for £250,000, in June 1976. That signing also broke the 13-year-old heart of a Blades fan named Vikki Orvice, who would go on to become my wife.

After their shocking start to the 74/75 season, Leeds had produced a strong finish to end up ninth in the First Division. It was, looking back, an amazing season in the English game, embracing so many disparate clubs contesting honours. Derby County won the title, with Ipswich Town, Stoke City, Sheffield United and Middlesbrough all within four points of them. Manchester United won the Second Division title after their previous season's relegation. West Ham lifted the FA Cup by beating Second Division Fulham in the final and the League Cup Final was contested by two Second Division sides in Norwich City and Aston Villa, both also promoted with Manchester United.

Over the next three seasons, during Jimmy's rebuild, Leeds finished fifth, tenth and ninth, reaching FA Cup and League Cup semi-finals in the process. Come the start of the 1978/79 season, Jimmy finally felt he had his own squad, one capable of challenging for honours. The board, however, now having recruited a couple of new directors wanting to put their own mark on the club, had other ideas.

After an end-of-season tour to Switzerland and a squad holiday playing golf in Marbella, Jimmy returned to find out from press gossip that the Leeds board were considering replacing him. He didn't believe it and confronted the board at its June meeting. The chairman Manny Cussins replied that he should start the season and that, when his contract was expiring in November, they would be keen to renew if he was doing well. Jimmy had also got wind from journalists that Cussins had been talking to the Celtic manager Jock Stein.

In the end, Jimmy made the decision for them. He had been enjoying managing the club – including the perk of being invited by York Minster to play the organ there. ('He loved it,' said Don Warters. 'He went two or three times.') But Jim was not going to stay where there were doubts about him.

CHAPTER 4

He was especially upset as he was about to view houses in Yorkshire, at last ready to move Anne, Duncan and John across from Blackpool. He felt that he was doing a good job on the field, and under his stewardship Leeds had gone from a £400,000 loss to a £250,000 profit. A new stand had been built as well.

'It was a bit sad the way it ended,' said Warters. 'Jimmy had done the job he was required to do. And he did it in a way that didn't upset people. Quietly and intelligently. He was a very intelligent man but not a soft touch. He was the first Leeds manager to substitute Billy Bremner. The whole stadium went quiet.' The journalist's assessment of Jim mirrored Paul Reaney's: 'He was very nice to deal with, but strong in his own way.'

John Armfield recalled the night his dad walked into the house after his final day at Elland Road: 'I remember him coming home with a painting he had on the wall of his office and a football he kept there. It was about the only time I can remember Mum and him having a row, or what for them was a row. She wondered why he'd just walked out but I think he'd been backed into a corner and he made a decision for the whole family. He wasn't going to move us over there without a new contract.'

'I think his attitude was that he had stuck with them and they should have stuck with him,' added Duncan. 'He'd given a lot to Leeds. It exhausted him. He'd drive an hour and 40 minutes there and back every day, and he loved it but he'd be terribly quiet in the evenings.'

In the days that followed, there were knocks at the door from journalists asking to speak to Jimmy but the family would tell them he wasn't available. It became so oppressive that Jimmy took them all off to Majorca for a fortnight until the news agenda moved on. And it soon did, as Leeds duly appointed Jock Stein. However, in a barely credible irony, he lasted only 44 days before resigning to take the Scotland job, Ally McLeod having lasted just one more game after Scotland's hapless World Cup in Argentina in the summer of 1978.

Jimmy's stock remained high and his autobiography told of offers from Leicester City, Blackburn Rovers, Newcastle, Chelsea, Heart of Midlothian and Athletic Bilbao. But a flame inside him had gone out. 'Leaving Leeds had upset me more than I allowed people to see,' he said. He did take on the England Under-18 job for a short while and, having regained some appetite for the role, according to Duncan, was about to take up the Iran national job until the revolution there in 1979. Any lingering desire to try his hand at management again was then doused when he applied for the Wales job eventually given to Mike England.

Before those episodes, however, and before Jimmy Adamson took over at Elland Road as Stein's successor, Duncan recalled there being a visitor. 'I remember Manny Cussins coming to the house and talking to Dad about him going back to Leeds. Dad said it was too late.' In *Right Back to the Beginning*, Jimmy revealed how Cussins phoned him on Christmas Day that year to lament that Jim had not sent him a Christmas card. Though he admitted to having the odd shouting match with Billy Bremner, not sending a card was probably the closest Jimmy would come to showing his displeasure with someone.

At times in the following years, Jimmy missed the company and camaraderie of players and the buzz of a training ground. With the approval of Blackpool managers, notably Sam Ellis and Jimmy Meadows, Jimmy would walk, run or cycle ('on the world's worst bike, with a red shopping bag on the back', said Duncan) from the Stony Hill Avenue house to the club's Squires Gate training ground and join in, sometimes taking charge of, and working with, the club's younger players.

I confess I felt a tug at a heartstring when I heard this. It reminded me of the sad story of Bill Shankly, seemingly regretting his retirement in 1974, walking down to the Liverpool training ground at Melwood to watch, unannounced, the players go through their paces before being requested – actually, instructed – by club officials to stay away. Instead, the great man took to going to the Everton training ground at Bellefield, where he was recruited to help coach youth teams.

Jimmy, never presumptuous, would not have gone without official sanction. And his humility of going from managing one of the country's great clubs to the youth teams of a lower-division set-up did not deter him. 'He just loved it,' said Duncan. 'He'd do all sorts to help out.'

CHAPTER 4

Thankfully, with any lingering ambitions of a return to management receding, Jimmy carved himself a new career in the media, one at which he excelled and in which he would become celebrated. His time learning the trade of sports journalism on the *Evening Gazette* at Blackpool would prove invaluable and soon the *Daily Express* offered him a job as a reporter on their Manchester sports desk. As a newspaperman at heart myself, I always admired Jim hugely for his willingness to do the real legwork and actually learn the trade. So many ex-players expect to be ghost-written, the journalist doing all the research and writing work unacknowledged while the player trousers a generous fee.

I remember once being in the Crystal Palace press box alongside the Chelsea and England striker Peter Osgood, who had just been taken on by the new knockabout tabloid the *Daily Sport* to cover matches. 'How much they paying?' another ex-pro nearby asked him. 'Twenty quid,' he replied. 'Twenty-five if you write it yourself.' I also recall another England captain, in an era after Jimmy, who was taken on to produce a column on a Sunday broadsheet. Initially, nobly, he wanted to write it himself before realising how difficult it was and requesting a ghost writer.

Jimmy had no such need. He once flew to Jersey, knocked on the mansion of Blackburn Rovers' moneybags owner Jack Walker and, through force of personality, secured a rare interview for the *Daily Express*.

But as good at writing for newspapers as he was, it was as a radio summariser and pundit alongside a commentator, first for BBC Radio 2 and later when Radio 5 Live was created in 1994, that Jimmy became – yes, I'm going to use the expression – a national treasure.

These days, there are seemingly more jobs than ever in broadcast media for ex-footballers, given the volume of coverage of the Premier League across a wide variety of outlets on commercial and public TV and radio. One of the key parts of the First Division's 1992 rebranding deal with Sky Sports was that the new satellite company had to offer significant support programming to live games, in the form of magazine content and air time for build-ups to games. It has since swollen to include Saturday-afternoon live updates and studio punditry across many platforms, providing a plethora of work opportunities.

Many such pundits appear to be there just to incense people or to manufacture talking points and to get people talking about the pundits themselves. Jimmy, who preceded this era and was on radio duty at the Hillsborough disaster in 1989, was never one of them. He was Lowryesque in painting pictures, with his honeyed, authoritative voice his brush; by contrast, many now are merely performing the equivalent of carving initials in trees with a kitchen knife. Where the voice used to be valued, now it is controversy and clicks that drive airwaves traffic. This is nothing to do with any snobbery about regional accents; Jimmy's was pure Lancastrian and perfect. It is to do with tone.

As well as tone of voice, the tone of his remarks was always appropriate. Not for him the cheap shot. He had been player, manager and journalist. He was generous and understanding, though never shirked his duty if a bad game needed to be described as such, a player and team's performance criticised or manager's selection questioned. This from Daniel Gray's book *Saturday, 3pm* is lyrical and accurate:

'Sometimes when Jimmy Armfield isn't speaking, I swear I can hear him smile. The radio commentator will have described a fine passage of play, and I just know that Jimmy is there, sitting back, arms folded, still enraptured by the game. ... While the content of Jimmy's words is in itself rich, delivery is key. His regular tone is soft but serious, a measured grandad explaining why stealing is wrong... It is reassuring, a handshake between England's old and new. Set against the jarring platitudes and rent-a-voices of other pundits, Jimmy is a nice cup of tea when all around us is Blue WKD.'

Jim was certainly generous to me when I crossed from being a production journalist, as deputy sports editor of *The Guardian*, to writer on the road, a young (well, youngish at 33), green buck in the late 1980s. We encountered each other regularly in press rooms and, even though he was spending the afternoon talking football on air, still he wanted to discuss the game, before and after. Clearly I was not alone in this. Jimmy was just like it with everyone. Many wanted to sit close, sipping tea with him, picking up his pearls as he sat conversing, his flat cap that would later fit under his headphones sitting on the table in front of him. I think we were all just hoping that the bonhomie rubbed off.

'We kept in touch and always made a point of having a chat whenever he came to Leeds to summarise,' Don Warters said. 'You couldn't have asked to spend time with a better person.'

All that said, Jimmy did have a little bit of an ego now and then. One Saturday, I was at Villa Park chatting to him with a group of other journalists and radio people. Some technical glitch had occurred at the game he was covering in midweek and he had been asked by the studio to contribute commentary, rather than just summarise alongside a commentator, for a couple of minutes to fill in while they fixed it.

'Did you hear my commentary?' Jimmy asked the group, eager as a puppy for a response. As it happened, I had, and said so.

'What did you think?' he said.

'Very vivid, Jim,' I replied.

'Did you hear that, lads?' he said. 'Vivid.' And that big smile came across his face.

I also recall a game at Highbury in the mid-1990s. George Graham, then Arsenal manager, had been revealed as having taken payments from an agent for signing two of the agent's players. It prompted the 'bungs' inquiry that saw Graham lose his job and others named but escape punishment.

In the press box, I was invited to contribute to a discussion about the revelation, sitting alongside Jimmy, with the commentator and correspondent Mike Ingham, another with the smoothest of radio voices and sharpest of eyes. I recall saying something about 'bodies in the box' being a footballing phrase and I hoped that Graham was not going to be the only body caught in the box given the scale of the wrongdoing likely to be revealed by the inquiry. I looked across the row and saw Jimmy smile at the phrase, this time more wryly, and nod. I had said something that had impressed Jimmy Armfield. How pleased I was with myself.

One of Jimmy's little quirks so beloved of those who knew him – most notably Mike Ingham, who used to log them – was his little 'what I call' moments. I emailed Mike, worthy successor to such radio football commentating greats as Peter Jones and Bryon Butler, asking for his recollections of 'Jimmyisms'.

'What I loved about them was that they defined understatement,' he wrote back. 'When he began the phrase you were anticipating some hold-the-back-page revelation, only to be treated to: "Thierry Henry, he's what I call a real handful", or "Martin Keown, he's what I call a no-nonsense defender".

'Of course they were never delivered unkindly or critically. I can just imagine him telling Bremner and Giles in the Leeds dressing room: "Gerd Muller – he's what I call a goalscorer!"

'My favourite "he's what I would call" from the great man was when he said to me in commentary about Aston Villa's Tony Morley: "He's what I would call a down-and-out winger!"'

And my own favourite? It comes from a Manchester United match, when the Dutchman Ruud van Nistelrooy scored with a clever lob. 'A lovely chip,' said Jimmy. 'That was what I would call a dinky-do.'

Mike also wrote of Jim in his own book, *After Extra Time and Penalties*: 'I probably worked with

Jimmy more than any other summariser and never once did he make it about himself and say anything for effect. It was always only about the game and, having been there himself as a distinguished player, he knew it was a tough profession and so was never over-critical, but everything he did say carried the weight of sage authority. I would look forward to a commentary even more than usual if I knew that Jimmy was going to be sitting alongside me.'

And then a terrible shock pulled up everyone in the game, and all those who followed it, when this wit and wisdom, charm and insight, came to a sudden stop in early 2007. He had been diagnosed with a throat cancer, non-Hodgkin lymphoma, at the age of 71. He disappeared off the airwaves, out of sight if not quite out of mind as he went through chemotherapy. I possibly took more note than many simply because my partner Vikki – not then yet my wife – had been diagnosed with secondary breast cancer at exactly the same time.

I waited until both had finished their stints of chemo, Vikki left exhausted and having lost her hair but making a recovery, before ringing Jimmy to check on him. I told him about Vikki and that I had seen at first hand the effects of the cancer and the treatment, both with her at the Royal Marsden Hospital in London and at home in the aftermath. I asked him how he was doing. Like Vikki, he said: exhausted, had lost his hair but was making a recovery. I asked if I could come up and see him.

'I'll tell you what,' he said. 'Give me a little bit longer and I'll let you have the first interview about it with me.'

5

VIKKI, HER hair growing back after finishing six rounds of monthly chemo and ready for a little trip, said she'd like to come with me to Blackpool. It was mid-October in 2007 and Jimmy had said that he felt he was now ready, physically and emotionally, to catch up with people properly again and would I like to come up and interview him? I'd absolutely bloody love to see you again, I said.

I had been with my employers at that point, the *Mail on Sunday,* for two years by then and they had been wonderful with me and for me. For Vikki, too. My sports editor, Malcolm Vallerius, had suggested just as Vikki was beginning chemo earlier that year that I take her with me to Cornwall for a few days extra around a feature I was writing for the paper. Now he told me again to book a nice hotel, have a couple of days of sea air rather than travel up and back in a day, take Vikki again and that the company would pay. I'd just been named Sports Journalist of the Year in the British Press Awards after a 2006 World Cup in Germany of comfortable hotels and efficient travel arrangements – and I remain convinced that such an attitude and treatment for the first time in my career, after working in broadsheets and doing things on the cheap for so long, helped me win the award as I only had to worry about my work.

We drove up the day before the interview and stayed at the Imperial. I think Vikki, from the Socialist Republic of South Yorkshire, liked the fact that famous Labour Party conferences had been held there. That evening, we drove slowly up from Lytham to Fleetwood so that she, still frail, could enjoy the celebrated Illuminations (which cost £1 extra on the room, I seem to remember, to help pay for them). The next morning, after breakfast, she said she'd like to come with me over to South Shore to Jimmy's house and maybe try and walk around a little while I interviewed him. If I left the car keys with her and she couldn't manage walking very far, she said, she could always come back and spread out on the back seat with a rug over her and indulge in her beloved pastime of reading a book while she waited for me. I was a little worried about leaving her, said I could interrupt the interview, take her back to a warm hotel room if she rang me on my mobile, but she said to stop fussing and she'd be fine. I was to tell Jimmy, by the way, that she still hadn't forgiven him for prising Tony Currie from Sheffield United 30 years previously.

As we drove along the seafront then turned off the main road and inland past the Pleasure Beach for my first visit to his home, I remember thinking that the whole area and atmosphere was so Jimmy: understated and unpretentious but homely. Where Premier League players now owned mansions in gated communities, or certainly behind gates in huge detached properties, Jimmy's house was detached but not huge, just neat and attractive, and unprepossessing.

We parked outside on leafy Stony Hill Avenue and I walked up to ring the bell, while Vikki sat in the front passenger seat of the car and decided what she was going to do next. Jimmy opened the door and he smiled. I'd missed that toothy smile in press rooms. I was immediately glad to see that he looked well. His hair, though thin and wispy, was returning and he had some colour in his face.

'All right, son? How are you?' he said.

'Good, thank you, Jimmy. More to the point, how are you?'

'Better than I was, that's for sure,' he said. 'Can't complain.'

He looked over my shoulder to see my car parked and somebody in the passenger seat.

'Who's that with you?' he asked.

'It's Vikki,' I replied.

'Well, don't leave her out there,' he said. 'Fetch her inside.'

In she came, with me grateful that she would be out of the autumn wind, and we sat in the kitchen for a while drinking tea, four of us, including Anne. Vikki and Jim compared cancer and chemo journeys, told their war stories. Jimmy wanted to know, above anything else, how it had all gone for her.

'How was your taste? Everything tasted metallic with me. When I could eat.'

'Yes. Same,' said Vikki.

'Did you lose all your hair?' he asked.

'Oh yes,' she said and smiled.

'Me too. Everywhere on my body,' he replied with a wider smile.

Anne then revealed that she'd had cervical cancer back in the day, and recovered fully.

'All sorts of things go through your mind, when you're young,' she said. 'How could I have got it? Was it through some, you know, activity? But I'd not been with anyone apart from Jim.'

'All right, all right,' Jimmy intervened. 'They don't need to know things like that.'

I can still picture Vikki looking across at me and smiling. Two years later, I too would contract a cancer, of the prostate, and the four of us would be further bonded. Not wishing to take up too much of Jimmy's time and tire him, I said we should get on with the interview but Vikki couldn't resist the moment, having been made to feel so at ease already in their company.

'By the way, Jimmy,' she said, the bluntness of her Yorkshire upbringing surfacing, 'I'm a Sheffield United fan and I'm still not happy with you for signing Tony Currie for Leeds.' She smiled to show she was joshing.

Jimmy returned a smile. 'My best signing,' he said.

We left Anne and Vikki chatting away and headed for his conservatory where we could sit and gaze out on the pride and joy that was his garden, the geraniums and roses now fading but clearly having been magnificent. He lamented that the lawn had not had its finest summer due to his 'incapacity'.

I asked him to take me through the timeline of it all, from the bleak February day when he was first diagnosed. I see him even now reaching for his green pocket FA diary on a side table, leafing through the pages.

'Blood test, scan, chemotherapy, radiotherapy,' he recited, matter-of-fact. 'These are usually football matches.'

Diagnosis of his throat cancer had, he said, been 'a defining moment'. Yet it took some while for it to arrive. He'd had a sore throat at those World Cup finals of June and July 2006 but thought little of it as he'd been prone to them all his life. The same when it returned at Christmas. Anne, however, urged him to see his doctor, who prescribed antibiotics. They didn't help. In January, he became aware of a lump having developed in his throat.

'It was huge,' he said, showing me the top of his thumb. 'As big as that. I knew something was wrong.'

He went to see an old friend, Andrew Keith, an ear, nose and throat specialist at Blackpool's Victoria Hospital on whose board Jimmy had served as a director for 12 years until the previous year. Suddenly, things moved quickly. Dr Keith recommended a biopsy and within 24 hours was standing on the Armfields' doorstep. Anne showed him into the living room, where he told Jimmy: 'It's bad news but it could be worse.' Within another couple of days, Jimmy was seeing an oncologist, Dr Marian 'Mac' Macheta, who insisted to him the cancer was eminently treatable.

Busy, busy Jimmy – involved in charities, football and a multitude of other activities – decided there was only one attitude to adopt. One course of action – or, rather, inaction. 'I do so many things but had to make a decision to concentrate on this,' he said. 'I just thought, "It has to be faced, and that's it." I wasn't frightened. If I had been 25 or 35, I might have been angry. I said to myself at the outset: "They are going to treat the illness and I am going to treat the treatment."'

There were three rounds of chemotherapy, each lasting all day. 'I always seemed to be the last one to leave,' he recalled. 'The staff were marvellous. They had a great sense of humour. The PFA rang me up and asked me if I wanted to go private but I was among good people. I just wanted to be in Blackpool.' It was always the way with Jimmy. It wasn't just the place; it was the people. He had affection for, and trust in, them.

In the three weeks between sessions, there were 16 steroid tablets a day to be taken, and visits back to hospital to boost the immune system. 'You don't go anywhere or do anything,' he said. As I saw with Vikki, and came to know with steroids myself, the treatment had a bloating and debilitating effect.

It had become public that Jimmy had cancer when his fellow 1966 World Cup squad member Alan Ball died suddenly and shockingly of a heart attack in the April that year at the age of just 61. Jimmy's absence at the memorial service at

Winchester Cathedral was noted and he decided to issue a statement. 'It upset me I couldn't make it to the service,' said Jimmy. 'Alan came to Blackpool as a lad at 16 and later we went on holiday with him and his wife and mum and dad.'

During his treatment and just after, Jimmy would have other shocks and sadnesses to endure too. John Schofield, vice-president of Blackpool FC, died of throat cancer, and Bill Perry, scorer of the injury-time winner after Mortensen's hat-trick in the 1953 FA Cup Final, also passed away with bowel cancer in the September. They had been in touch throughout each other's treatment. 'There's been one or two downers along the way,' he lamented to me, the understatement hanging in the air, the stoicism of his generation evident again.

When Jimmy's cancer did become public, the response was astonishing. Bouquets arrived, first from the FA, then some 400 cards and 2,500 emails. Sir Bobby Robson, who would die from a cancer that had spread to multiple sites two years later, was a regular telephone caller.

Jimmy's mobile certainly rang plenty after the League One play-off final in the May. Naturally, he would have loved to have been at Wembley to see Blackpool beat Yeovil Town to reach the Championship. Instead, he was shivering, in pyjamas and dressing gown, in front of an open, roaring fire even though the spring bank holiday weather was warming up early-season holidaymakers in the town. 'Get Well Jim' read T-shirts revealed by the Blackpool players after the victory. 'It was quite emotional,' Jimmy said, trying not to repeat the emotion, the silence afterwards telling of it, though.

The conclusion of the chemo was tough, a mix of anticipation and trepidation. 'You don't feel like going for the last one, but you've got to go,' he said. 'When they talk about battling cancer, that's what they mean.'

It did not represent an end to the physical privations, however, and indeed there would be many more. The chemo had shrunk the tumour but did not rid him of all traces of the cancer. There was radiotherapy yet to be endured, to mop up residual cells around the original site, though he needed a blood transfusion in a Preston hospital before he was strong enough to endure 15 consecutive weekdays of it.

'I was very weak. It wasn't easy for me to get out to the car and I didn't say anything all morning while I was there,' he recalled. After the transfusion though? 'By the evening, I could have walked home.' Having also been fitted for a mask to cover face and shoulders and which would protect against the radiotherapy's beams, he felt ready for whatever came next.

'I said, "I'm fine, just do it." That was my attitude. I just closed my eyes and this big machine went round my face and my head, back and front. I kept thinking to myself, "This must be doing me good." The first two weeks were OK but I remember the third week. The young doctor brought in a 1966 World Cup programme for me to sign and I said, "You get me through this and I'll sign it."

'I said to him that the initial cancer was very painful, like having toothache and earache at the same time, and it can't be any more painful than that. But it was. I still had the attitude that this was going to get me right. I had blisters and sores in my mouth, my lips were swollen. The back of my neck was burning. You just had to grit your teeth. After that, I was living off soup, custard, rice pudding, sago and protein drinks.'

Gradually he began to feel stronger again, enough to venture out, first to familiar places he really missed and that brought instant comfort. He played the organ again at St Peter's – 'very therapeutic' – and made it to a game at Bloomfield Road, against Colchester United, where he was asked to do the half-time raffle ticket draw.

'I was just going to do the draw but the applause went on for five minutes and I felt I had to say something,' he recalled. 'I'm not normally stumped for words when I get behind a microphone but it was a moving moment because everybody was still standing. I told them I'd had some dark days but hopefully they were behind me. The applause started again and went on for another three minutes. Half-time was coming to an end and I hadn't even done the draw.'

The new Wembley had been opened in the March just as Jimmy was embarking on his treatment and he had been disappointed at missing the big England game against Brazil there in the June. He would make it back for the game against

Croatia the month after our interview, though. And back to the microphone, to reach 30 years of broadcasting, for Bolton Wanderers v Aston Villa the week after we spoke.

I asked him if he had ever been worried about the effect of all the treatment on his throat, and thus his voice. The answer was pure Jimmy: 'It never entered my head,' he said. 'I've never been worried about myself. People have mentioned about my voice being distinctive but you don't think about your own voice. I've never, ever felt sorry for myself and I never thought, "Well, this is it," because I've seen other people come through. And I was never frightened, even when I was bald and pale. I just wasn't going to look in the mirror. That's one thing about getting older. Your vanity goes. I still feel there are more chapters.'

Our interview had reached a natural conclusion after about an hour and I didn't want to tire him, but he had one last thing he wanted to say.

'I don't want you to use the word hero,' he said. 'I am no different to anyone else.' All these years later, I hope he would permit me the title of this book.

On the way into the house, I had noticed some mementoes of his life in and out of football, though he insisted he was never a great hoarder of memorabilia.

I asked him now if I could have a closer look and Vikki and Anne joined us. There was the shield proclaiming James C Armfield, Sheriff of Lancashire, certificates showing his OBE, awarded in 2000 for services to football, and the freedom of Blackpool. A portrait of him in his prime as a footballer in the distinctive tangerine hung from a wall.

But it was the glass cabinet that held most attraction. Beneath medals and ribbons were Jimmy's gorgeous 43 blue felt England caps, so evocative to this young boy growing up. And so precious, so beautiful. On top of the collection was the one for the 1962 World Cup quarter-final between Brazil and England.

'We lost 3-1,' he said. (Of course I knew, recalling my seven-year-old self with my football magazines, but that was Jimmy's modesty – he would not presume that people knew of him and his achievements.) 'But at 1-1 it was anybody's game. We missed two or three very good chances. I was so lucky. I really did play in a golden era with England.'

For many years since that visit, memory insisted that it was me who asked the next question. As time has progressed, however, I reckon it might well have been Vikki. Whoever it was, it certainly became a significant moment for both Jimmy and me.

'Can we see your 1966 World Cup medal?' I/ she said.

'We didn't get them,' Jimmy replied. 'Only the 11 who played in the final got them.'

I remember looking at Vikki and her looking at me. We were both stunned.

'Really?' I said. 'I can't believe that, Jim.'

I had read somewhere that at the previous year's World Cup, the finalists Italy and France had each received 46 medals. Even press officers were getting them. Now I discovered that players who had played in group matches – Jimmy Greaves, John Connelly, Ian Callaghan and Terry Paine – let alone those who played a huge part in helping to get the team into shape, physically and mentally, those such as Jimmy Armfield, did not get World Cup winners' medals.

I was not just stunned. I was disgusted.

'That's how it was,' Jimmy said and shrugged his shoulders. Some years later when I finally read his autobiography, I discovered in it his disappointment on behalf of his fellow back-up players that they had not received medals, but today, here and now, he was not going to complain to a journalist.

Vikki and I thanked Anne and Jim for tea, their time and their generosity of conversation. I shook hands with him (Jimmy was not of the man-hug generation), and we got into the car to head back south to our home in Hertfordshire.

'What a lovely man,' Vikki said. 'And Anne's lovely too. You know, I think I might finally forgive him for Tony Currie. Only might, mind.'

I looked across at her as I drove to the M55 and can still picture her smile. I told her I had an idea that I was going to take back to my sports editor at the *Mail on Sunday*. She said she thought it was a cracking idea. Vikki always did have a good eye and instinct for these things.

6

THERE'S AN old slice of newspaper wisdom that says that you don't start a campaign unless you know you're going to win it. It's a bit like barristers in court never asking a question unless they know the answer to it. The risk of surprises and humiliation is simply too great.

My sports editor was definitely up for this one, though. 'It's a no-brainer, surely?' he said. It had to be, I replied. How could any campaign to secure medals for England's back-up squad of 1966 possibly fail?

And so, alongside my big interview with Jimmy in the sports pages of the *Mail on Sunday* that weekend, there appeared a story that we were going to petition the game's authorities in order to make it happen.

After interviewing Jimmy, I'd spent much of the rest of the week phoning people, having planned a strategy with Vikki on the drive back from Blackpool. First stop was the sports minister, Richard Caborn. He and Vikki had much in common, starting with their home city and support for Sheffield United. He was closely involved with the 2012 Olympic Games and its delivery, as was Vikki in her role as athletics correspondent of *The Sun* to accompany her job as a football reporter. The Games had been awarded to London back in 2005 in Singapore and Lord Sebastian Coe would later pay tribute to Vikki for getting her employers on board, almost a necessity back in those days when the paper was reaching ten million readers a day. Not only was Richard one of Vikki's great contacts, he had become a friend.

I had piggybacked that and he had given me several interviews down the years. I outlined the idea to him. He was immediately on board. 'What a great plan,' he said. 'Count me in.' As a politician, he recognised that there was no downside to this. It would be popular, non-controversial and highly likely to succeed. He gave me quotes backing the initiative and would, he said, immediately contact Sepp Blatter. Then the most powerful man in world football as head of FIFA, Blatter was a figure not to everyone's taste, as proved when he was forced to resign amid financial investigations in 2015, but he could make this happen.

Next, I phoned the FA's head of media Adrian Bevington and he also agreed it was something the English game's governing body could get behind. Again, there would be no cost to them and no adverse ramifications. We were gathering immediate momentum.

Before we went to print, I phoned Jimmy again. I didn't want to do anything to embarrass him, I said. He had, he repeated, long believed that 'my lot' deserved to be recognised and he would, privately and silently, be very happy for my newspaper to instigate a campaign to reward his fellow reserves. It was just that he didn't want to be seen to be getting involved with it. I understood. Pushing himself forward was not Jimmy's style.

I also got a number for Jimmy Greaves and rang him. Yes, he was willing to be quoted as backing the plan, he said, mainly for the other 'chaps'. In all honesty, though, he was not overly excited about the prospect of a retrospective medal. If I wanted to do it, that would be nice, he added, but it was all a long time ago and he wasn't going to be bothered one way or the other. It was clear from the tone of his voice that old wounds were still deep. If anything, though, his reaction only fired me up to want to go ahead with this. I could do something worthwhile for my boyhood hero, hoping that it would help seal, if not heal, those wounds.

Blatter quickly embraced the idea when Richard Caborn contacted him. In fact, he liked it so much that within a month he had decreed that all squad members of World Cup finalists, going back to the very first tournament, in Uruguay in 1930, would be awarded medals – managers and trainers as well. Where they had passed on, the medals were to be awarded posthumously and presented to members of their family. Clearly our Sepp knew a path to popularity when he saw it.

After that, however, the wheels of FIFA ground slowly. I would check with Richard every few months to see how we were doing and sometimes write another story updating the campaign to keep the pressure on. I desperately had to find a new angle to justify it with my sports editor – such as getting a major footballing figure to say that it was a scandal that it hadn't happened before, and that the situation should be rectified as soon as possible. We needed action to follow up those early encouraging words from Blatter. Most of these England players were in their seventies now and I wanted them to have their moment in person.

Then, in the spring of 2009, about 18 months after I had written the first article, word came via Richard that FIFA were ready to strike the medals and see them presented. I was utterly delighted, and so was Jimmy when I rang to tell him.

'It's good news. I'm glad,' he said for an article for the paper. 'It's been a long wait. People asked me over the years if I was disappointed but I wasn't really. In those days it was accepted that only those who played in the final got the medals. Life was different. It was a harsher regime. But you see everyone these days getting medals and it made you wonder. Now it's coming it will be nice. I'm sure all those lads who did play in the final will appreciate the gesture for those who didn't. Some of them played in earlier games.'

He was, he added, particularly pleased for the relatives of Sir Alf Ramsey, his assistant Harold Shepherdson and the trainer Les Cocker. 'They served England well for a long time and it's something for their families to hand down.'

Soon, with Adrian Bevington pulling out the stops, the FA were organising a presentation of the players at Wembley ahead of an England match, a World Cup qualifying game against Andorra, the following month. Richard Caborn went even further. He persuaded the then Prime Minister Gordon Brown to host a reception at 10 Downing Street for them. Apart from one pool reporter and a photographer from a news agency, I was to be the only journalist allowed into the room when the PM presented the medals.

I thought back to being 11 years old, in our small terraced house in Weymouth, and the day of the World Cup Final of 1966. It was our moving day, from rented accommodation to my parents' first owned house. The first thing off the van was the black-and-white TV so we could switch it on to make sure it was warmed up in plenty of time, as had to be done in those days, before it yielded a picture. I remember our hearts being in mouths, worrying that it would be corrupted by lines across the screen that required careful manipulation of the horizontal and vertical hold buttons. But it worked. Eventually, we could perch on boxes to watch the final.

Now, as somebody who had helped deliver some measure of justice for them, I was going to be in a room with a group of men all of whom would have been good enough to play in that final – who were, indeed, major participants in the event and the day. I grew emotional at the very prospect, even starstruck despite having been a Fleet Street sports journalist for almost 30 years by that point and having met many major figures.

We were all to meet up for a light lunch at the Royal Lancaster Hotel overlooking Hyde Park ahead of the Downing Street reception and England's game against Andorra on Tuesday 10 June. It was wonderful to see Anne there, along with all the other players' wives. I was indeed rendered a fan boy at the sight of such men as Ian Callaghan and

Norman Hunter. And of course the two Jimmys –
Greaves and Armfield – my heroes of youth and
middle age. These figures may have gone unnoticed
in the street today but they were national giants of
my childhood and adolescence. It was especially
heart-warming to see Sir Geoff Hurst and Roger
Hunt, who had played on 30 July 1966, join the
group to lend support and rekindle old friendships.
The right-back who had replaced Jimmy, George
Cohen, was here to represent Lady Vickie, Sir Alf
Ramsey's widow – how scandalous that not even
the manager had received a winners' medal. Family
members representing Harold Shepherdson and Les
Cocker, both also now deceased, were here too.

(Jimmy once told me that for many years, the
whole 1966 squad and wives would meet at a hotel
with a golf course for an annual weekend reunion.
I beseeched him to ask if they would let me come to
write a big piece about it but he didn't want anyone
from outside to intrude on the magic. The journalist
in me was disappointed. The man, who was no part
of it nor deserved to be, understood fully.)

After the lunch, it would be on to Downing
Street for the reception before heading to Wembley

in plenty of time for a meal at the stadium and a presentation of the players on the pitch to the crowd ahead of kick-off. It wouldn't quite work out that way, however, for London that day was at the mercy of a Tube strike.

We were already late because journalists – bloody journalists – had been invited to the hotel pre-lunch for interviews and the players had given their all, notably Jimmy G, the most in demand. What should have been a 20-minute journey on the plush England Under-23 coach that we'd been allocated for the day took more than an hour and the day's schedule was now torn up. (Jimmy G, his wit still sharp to confirm his TV persona for years alongside Ian St John in the hugely popular show *Saint and Greavsie*, was quick with a quip. 'Blimey,' he said. 'Charabancs have changed since my day.')

Even before the players passed through the famous black door, they were in demand for more photos from the ever-present bank of TV and still cameramen positioned opposite No. 10. News correspondents there on all-day duty, and probably instructed by their rolling-news offices to get something while they were waiting for political stories, wanted more interviews with Jimmy G. As he finally crossed the threshold, Norman Hunter put an arm round him. 'That,' said Greaves at the gesture, 'is the closest we have ever been without you scarring me.'

It seemed Jimmy A was the only one to have been to Downing Street before, as a boy on a school trip to London. Now, thick security gates separate the seat of government from the entrance to the street off Whitehall, but Jimmy recalled back then being able to wander up and stand in front of the door with his schoolmates to see its comings and goings. 'I think Attlee was Prime Minister,' he said.

A hush came over the group as they entered the celebrated black-and-white tiled hallway and were shown up the stairs where on the yellow walls hung all the portraits of previous Prime Ministers. George Cohen remarked that Gladstone and Disraeli may be close to each other now but they hated each other back in the day.

Once into a large reception room, the players gathered on the far side. I decided to take a position opposite, discreetly in a corner by a door, not realising that the Prime Minister would be bounding through that door. And when he did, I quickly became aware of the difference between Gordon Brown and his Labour predecessor, Tony Blair.

Vikki had been in Singapore in 2005 when Blair appeared at a reception for International Olympic Committee members hosted by the London bid team ahead of the vote on the city to be awarded the 2012 Games. He worked the room incessantly, she told me, going from one IOC member to another, targeting the waverers between London and their closest rivals, Paris. He was briefed well, yes, but he also retained a wealth of information about each delegate – the sport they specialised in, details of their family members – and asked them about their lives. It was all largely unseen but no doubt influential in London ultimately winning the vote.

Today, by contrast, Brown suddenly appeared alone through the door and held out his hand towards the first person he encountered. Which happened to be me. 'Hello,' he said. 'I'm Gordon Brown.' I smiled and accepted the handshake before he spotted the players in the opposite corner of the room and headed for them, Jimmy G first. Though

I had always been impressed by Brown's seriousness as a politician and his long period of competence as Chancellor, this was a moment that demonstrated that he simply did not have Blair's easy charisma. Indeed, the following year the voting public would decide that David Cameron had more of it, even if he did need the Liberal Democrats to shore him up.

Nevertheless, Brown's often suppressed warmth and engaging manner once initial shyness was overcome was evident as he relaxed into the afternoon after presenting the medals. I think it was Jimmy G who noted that probably the Prime Minister and John Connelly were the only left-wingers in the room. Brown would be accused by some newspapers of using the occasion for political popularity, but it was uncharitable and not what I witnessed. He was acceding to a request by Richard Caborn, also present, to put the most famous house in the country at the disposal of a group of its great sporting heroes. It was, quite simply, fitting. And his short speech was spot on.

'Justice has finally been done,' he said. 'I have watched your careers and noted that when you retired from football, you remained great servants to your country. You made history by showing that England could host and win a World Cup. It is because of you and your legacy that we are able to bid for 2018.'

That didn't go too well and Russia would win the vote.

Tea, coffee and neat little sandwiches were served, and we were allowed to wander through a few rooms and walk out on to a balcony that overlooked the splendid gardens. There, I found myself next to the Prime Minister once more.

'I thought you did very well not to mention Scotland winning 3-2 at Wembley in England's first match after the 1966 World Cup,' I said.

'Yes,' he replied, 'very restrained, wasn't I?' And any facial austerity of which he had been regularly accused disappeared into a warm and broad smile.

After more photos in Downing Street – and I still treasure mine on the back of this book with Jimmy A, he in his PFA tie, and those with Anne and Richard Caborn taken for the *Mail on Sunday* – it was back on the coach for Wembley. Once more, London traffic on the day of a Tube strike put paid to timings and it took no less than three hours to cover the nine miles and reach the national stadium, the Embankment particularly choked. It at least gave plenty of opportunity for reminiscences. And for studying the medals, 43 years in the making – so tiny, but precious, 5cm gold discs in wooden boxes. One or two players and their wives, it has to be said, noted with disappointment that these were not replicas of the medals awarded to the first team on the day but were more commemorative versions. Most seemed not to mind too much, or at least declined to voice it if they did.

A conversation began about how Alf had called the reserve players down from the stands five minutes before the end of normal time with England leading 2-1 so that they would be there at the final whistle as part of the celebrations. Wolfgang Weber's equaliser postponed that notion, however, and so they had to find vantage points for extra time wherever they could. Jimmy A stood with Jimmy G at the side of the benches for the team officials. Jimmy A and Norman Hunter recalled their superstitions – the one man wearing that red V-neck sweater to match the colour of England's shirts that day, the other carrying his raincoat over an arm – so as to repeat their apparel and behaviour for the team's first win of the tournament, the group match against Mexico.

Ian Callaghan remembered that Nobby Stiles had asked him to keep his false teeth in his jacket pocket, ready to hand over so that the little terrier would look presentable when meeting the Queen. All self-consciousness was lost in the euphoria of extra-time victory, however, and they remained in Callaghan's pocket, Stiles's toothless joy entering folklore.

There had been a story that Jimmy G went with Bobby Moore to the Playboy Club on Park Lane that night, with Jimmy A and all their wives accompanying them too. Jimmy G claimed, playfully probably, to have no memory of going there: 'Jimmy Armfield in the Playboy Club? If you'd said Jimmy and church, it might have rung a bell.'

Jimmy A spoke up, saying that he had been delighted to receive his OBE for services to football in 2000 and that he really thought everyone else in the squad who didn't have one ought to get one.

That should be the next campaign, he said, and he himself might try and start it.

I asked Jimmy G if I could have five minutes privately with him in one of the spare seats at the back of the bus and he agreed. I wanted to ask *the* question, and I felt it was my duty as a working journalist that day to do so.

'Can you tell me about the hurt of the final, Jim?' I asked.

It produced the most poignant moment of this momentous day, a smidgen of sorrow still in his eyes and a wistfulness in his voice now. It took around 15 long seconds for him to answer, during which I wondered whether I had spoiled the day.

'It was devastating for me that I didn't play in the final,' he said. 'I always believed that we would win the World Cup and I'd be part of it. But I wasn't. It wouldn't have been so important now because I would have been a substitute and probably would have got on.'

I thanked him for his candour and commiserated with him. Told him that he had been my boyhood hero. He thanked me for saying that, and for all I had done. It was a moment to treasure and one that will always stay with me.

I'd had my answer and it was a moment not to be dwelt upon on such a day, nor a time to press for more about the years that ensued, about the alcoholism and the once light-footed, elegant thoroughbred ending his career in sad circumstance in non-league football at Barnet. I later remembered that, as a student, I managed to get some stewarding work at an indoor event in London in the mid-1970s, where veteran stars of capital clubs would play ex-players from other cities. Jimmy struggled, overweight, and it pained me to see him sinking pint after pint in the bar afterwards. Thankfully, he found his way back to us again through sobriety (I have a lovely mug with a picture on it of he and Bobby Moore drinking tea) and demonstrate his talent for football insight and fun to new generations. He finally passed away aged 81 in 2021 having lived with the effects of a stroke for six years.

Wembley was finally approaching but so too was kick-off and the players' presentation to the crowd would have to wait until half-time (when

Jimmy G appeared on national television and surprised the interviewer by giving an honest, rather than diplomatic, assessment of England's current crop, who won 6-0 on the night but did not wholly impress him. It was a wry, dry and trenchant critique that showed us what less brave and over-earnest modern TV punditry was missing.) Naturally Wembley warmed to them as they stood waving from the pitch. It was an emotional moment for me too, now high up in the press box. Most of my fellow journalists were understandably off in search of refreshment but I was grateful to the one next to me applauding and congratulating me on my efforts on these players' behalf.

Before we got off the bus, I had asked Jimmy G how he now felt about today, having initially been lukewarm. Yes, he said, it had been better than he expected. He was in good spirits too, he added, because he had just met his first great-grandchild, a 9lb boy.

'I don't think any of us expected to get a medal, nor did we want one,' he said. 'But when I heard we were finally getting them, I thought, "That's great for the lads. Let's enjoy it and have a good day." And that's how it's been.'

Over the following years, some of the group would sell their medals at auction and I confess to having mixed feelings about it. When Terry Paine, who had come over from his home in South Africa for the Downing Street reception, sold his in 2011 for £27,500, I was phoned by a couple of media outlets asking how I felt. I was, in all honesty, a little disappointed. Medals – rarely awarded back then as this whole episode confirms – had meant a huge amount to me as a budding young follower and player of sport but I was not in the league of these guys who had won so much, probably had enormous collections of memorabilia, and were now at a stage of their lives where the money was more useful to them and their families. It was not about my disappointment, nor me. I simply said it was up to the players themselves what they did with their medals. And of course it was.

Probably because I felt so warmly towards Jimmy Greaves, I was actually pleased for him when he got £44,000 for his in 2014 while he was still active and able to enjoy the money. It came at an auction and on a day when the first team's left-back Ray Wilson's original went for £136,000. By now I was just pleased that I had helped him, or his family, in some way.

As for Jimmy A, he was never going to let his go. That day at Downing Street, caressing the medal in his hand, he told me that he was due to give a talk at a school in Blackpool a few days after the reception and it would be going with him for all the young students to see, handle and question him about. That was Jimmy Armfield's reaction to it all. But then we're all different and we all have our back stories, experiences that guide our attitudes and behaviours, and roles in the world. I loved them both but Jimmy A was my hero now that I was an adult more interested if not in the meaning of life, then in giving life some meaning. And, with my life enriched by his friendship, I would become even closer to him after that day.

7

IN THE summer of 2010, a year after our day at Downing Street, I found myself in Jimmy's conservatory drinking tea again, interviewing him once more about another joyous event. I'd covered the Championship play-off final at Wembley a few months earlier in which Blackpool had beaten Cardiff City, a wonderful free kick by Charlie Adam the pick of the goals in a 3-2 win. Now the *Mail on Sunday* magazine *Live* had sent me up to the town again to write a feature on the Premier League's latest member. A club that had dropped out of the top flight the year of Jimmy's retirement as a player was finally back after 39 years. The place was buzzing. Jimmy was buzzing.

I was there to poke and probe about the town for background and colour, to interview the then chairman and major shareholder, Karl Oyston.

He had reluctantly begun to run the club in the wake of a scandal when his father Owen was sent to prison for three years, convicted of raping a model attached to a talent agency in which he had a financial stake.

'The day after we won promotion, the Premier League rang me and said they wanted to meet with our eight heads of department,' said Karl Oyston. 'I said, "We don't have eight departments, let alone eight heads."'

Now all seemed settled, a huge adventure about to unfold, with Karl having attracted investment from a Latvian businessman by the name of Valeri Belokon, who had acquired 25 per cent of the club from Owen. Belokon's money had enabled them to buy Charlie Adam for £500,000 and the new investor had worn a tailor-made tangerine-coloured suit at Wembley.

They also had a cheery, chummy manager in Ian Holloway who had secured promotion on a limited budget and against all the odds. I went to see him in his Portakabin office at the underwhelming training ground, where written on a whiteboard in felt tip was a list of transfer targets that he asked me not to include in my article. Even if his voice was deep Bristolian burr, with his own back story of adversity – having helped his wife Kim through lymphatic cancer and three of his four children having been born deaf – Holloway seemed to fit Blackpool perfectly.

'Well,' he said, 'we both look better in the dark.'

'He's bright and breezy, like the town,' said Jimmy over that tea in his conservatory, though he didn't want to glaze over some of the unhappier facts of the place. 'I was an NHS director here for 14 years and the Victoria is a good hospital but you do see a lot of health issues,' he said. 'And we do have job problems.' Soon, however, he'd be telling me all about the investment going into the place – to spruce up the promenade, to improve the tram route.

Alas, his and the town's euphoria would last only a season and Blackpool were relegated. It had been fun while it lasted. Jimmy remained philosophical. He'd seen so much before, known the ups and downs of football, especially in his years as Leeds manager. Over the next few years, the club would unravel. It emerged that Owen Oyston had been paid £11m from Premier League money coming into the club, to the disgust of Blackpool fans and other followers of the game more widely. Karl and Valeri Belokon entered an acrimonious dispute about ownership.

Jimmy grew sad at all the goings-on. He was asked many times to comment, to take sides, but he never would. He just shook his head, a disappointment in his eyes. He was right to remain impartial. My own view was that he was above it all, and too good for both parties. Blackpool duly went into freefall, to League Two within six seasons, and Karl Oyston was ordered to pay £31m to Belokon. A new owner finally took over in 2019 and Blackpool won promotion back to the Championship.

For several years after that Premier League season, mine and Jimmy's friendship coincided mostly at games we were both covering, when we'd catch up, both fully paid-up members of the Cancer Club, my own having returned and spread in the early autumn of 2012. He'd ask me about Vikki and how she was getting on. Now a freelance, I'd also ring him for the odd quote for a piece – and, looking back, I think he may well have rung me with that Leeds/Chelsea European semi-final link to help me out.

We also sat and talked when a newspaper sent me up to cover the first Preston North End game after the death of the legendary Sir Tom Finney in February of 2014, aged 91. Jimmy told of Finney's athleticism, of how thoughtful and considerate, modest and humble a man he was. Like Jim, he had been a one-club man, even though he'd once had a lucrative offer to go to Italy, which would have meant him giving up his job as a plumber with his own business. Another son of Lancashire, Finney also believed that there was no place like home and he enjoyed the interaction with the public his work gave him.

No wonder, then, that Finney and Armfield had been close friends. As Jimmy used to say to his sons: 'The reason for travel is coming back to Blackpool.' And it was no surprise that Jimmy was asked to deliver a eulogy at Sir Tom's funeral at Preston Minster where, wearing his FA tie, he told the congregation: 'I am just pleased to have been on the same planet at the same time as him.'

That match day at Preston, ahead of a 0-0 draw, I told Jimmy that I'd seen the Preston team of Finney's day described once as 'the plumber and ten drips'. He smiled, liked it, but was never going to pass comment, having too much respect for any professional player who made it into a top club's first team.

That day also gave me another idea. Back in the New Year's Honours list of 2010, Jimmy had been awarded a CBE, an upgrade on his OBE, for his services to the community in Lancashire. John remembers getting a phone call from his dad in the autumn of 2009 about the CBE, being told to keep it quiet.

'What's all that noise in the background?' John asked.

'It's traffic.'

'So where are you?'

'I'm at the bus stop, going to the church.'

Here was a newly ennobled Commander of the British Empire, standing at a bus stop on his way to practise his organ playing.

While a CBE is a highly significant award and recognition, I always felt that Jimmy had deserved a knighthood for his remarkably varied services both to football, including broadcasting, and a wider world of charity and community. I decided to download the nomination form from a government website.

I did everything required. I gathered press cuttings about him, testimonials, and assembled them into a package. Three relevant people had to back and sign the application and I had little trouble in persuading Gordon Taylor, chief executive of the PFA, Tony Adams, former Arsenal and England captain and an old friend, along with Mark Pougatch, BBC Radio 5 Live presenter, to add their weight to the cause. And… nothing. I never heard a thing back. More importantly, Jimmy never did become a Sir. I never told him about any of it, of course, because he would have been embarrassed. Yet I continued to feel – no matter one's views on the honours system – that if anyone deserved a knighthood as an example of all that was good about the country, it was Jimmy Armfield.

Anyway, in the mid-2010s, with us both in remission, there was little occasion apart from us both being at games to talk about any cancer issues.

We were both just working and getting on with our lives – Jimmy enjoying his grandchildren while Vikki and I, now married, were making the most of things amid all the pills and potions we both took. Mine had helped keep me stable. Vikki's cancer was more virulent than mine, and her medications and treatments would work for a while but then she'd need a new chemo or radiotherapy every other year. She used to joke that our bathroom cabinet looked like it belonged to a Russian field event athlete.

Then it all changed in November 2016. Jimmy's cancer returned and he required an operation. For a tumour on his neck, I later discovered. After hearing the news, I gave it a week and phoned him.

'It's not good. I'm not good,' he said. 'I've got no energy. How's you and Vikki?'

'We're doing OK, thanks, Jim,' I said. 'But tell me more about you.'

'Well, I'm annoyed I can't get to Wembley for Blackpool next week,' he said, referring to the League Two play-off final against Exeter City that they would win 2-1, heralding their return to better days and a higher level. I wanted to get up to see him.

'I'm not feeling great,' he said. 'Ring me after Christmas and we'll see how I am.'

I frequently did during 2017, which would prove to be Jimmy's final complete year – one with a litany of cancer-related conditions, procedures, operations to remove tumours and treatments that debilitated and drained him. That year brought four more surgeries. There would be one via keyhole on his scalp under local anaesthetic lasting three hours and another to excise a growth on the top of an ear. Another was to remove affected lymph nodes in his throat as well as what his son Duncan called 'the big one', lasting six hours, to remove another rapidly growing tumour on his neck. The day following that, Jimmy had a stroke, though he recovered enough to keep up his regular telephone conversations.

It was astonishing how matter-of-fact and accepting he was of every onslaught of brutality that assailed him. But while there was no self-pity in his voice, come the summer, there was an understandable melancholy about him that I heard for possibly the first time.

'I'm a bloody mess,' he said. 'Can't play the piano, can't read. A real bloody mess. At least I can still stand on my own two feet at the moment. I don't know what to do or think. I get a bit dispirited now and then but I don't feel as sick as I did.'

But, he added, there was something that was about to cheer him up.

'That's one good thing,' he said. 'Football's coming back.'

'Still loving it then, Jim?' I asked.

'Oh yes,' he replied.

I recalled another charming passage from Daniel Gray's *Saturday, 3pm*: 'When I hear Jimmy Armfield's voice I feel like I am listening in on an impromptu love letter to the game. He may only be describing a dubious offside decision, but it comes from such a tender place that I can't help but be moved.

'Armfield remains bewitched and besotted after a lifetime of football: there is hope for us all.'

The Brazilian Neymar had just joined Paris Saint Germain from Barcelona for £200m and the deal was exercising Jim.

'I can't believe it,' he said. 'Well, actually I can. It looks nonsensical but they'll know what they're doing these money men. There'll be instalments and clauses if he gets injured after a week. I always question what these huge fees do to the players themselves. You find out a lot about their character.'

Having been through so much, and feeling so ill, still he wanted to talk football. It was, I suppose, his way of trying to retain a semblance of normality in a life that was otherwise now about medical matters. I suspect it was also an attempt to take himself away from the confines of his home to a wider world. A year later, I came to see it too with Vikki, who was determined to slip the shackles of her ever-worsening illness whenever she could, even to travel when it permitted.

'I'll pop up soon, Jimmy, eh?' I said.

'Ring me in a month,' he said again. 'See how I'm doing then.'

I did. Vikki and I were having a short early-autumn break in Norfolk and I just felt like calling him after a long, beautiful walk. For some reason, Holkham beach had put me in mind of Blackpool sands.

'I'm doing a lot better than when you last spoke to me,' he said. 'I can eat and walk about but I can't really get out. I don't go anywhere.' He and Anne had a static caravan by the side of Lake Windermere that had long been a bolthole between football seasons and where they took the boys when younger. They all loved it and it pained him that they couldn't get up there.

'You live in Blackpool, Jim,' I said, trying to console him. 'You're always on holiday.' I heard a little chuckle down the line.

'Yes, I suppose I am,' he said. 'Eh, what about that lad Woodburn? What's his background?'

Wales had played a World Cup qualifier the night before against Austria and the teenager Ben Woodburn had scored a wonderful goal, which Jimmy said he had witnessed before falling asleep in front of the television. We discussed him, talked about him being in the Liverpool academy.

'Anyway,' said Jimmy, 'I'm OK. Just waiting to hear about my next treatment.'

'Shall I come up, Jim?'

'It's a long way for you, and the weather's on the turn.'

I said OK, that I'd ring again soon. After the call ended, Vikki, who had been listening, suggested that perhaps Jimmy didn't want me to see him in his current condition, that he might be embarrassed or want only his family around. That made sense all of a sudden and I understood. Knowing Jimmy, it was not about vanity but about potential awkwardness on the part of a visitor at his current weakness and memories possibly being sullied, even though they could never be for me.

And so there were more phone calls. I always knew I would be just one among many and used to wonder how many Jimmy received in a day, so much in demand was he, so many well-wishers, friends and contacts did he have. Much bigger fry than me, too, though he had the knack of according everyone the same attention.

'The phone was always ringing,' said Duncan. 'A lot of Premier League managers would call him. He spoke to David Moyes a lot. They got on well. And Sir Alex Ferguson. So many people would ask him for advice and he'd offer it freely. Never once did he ask for money.'

John remembered one particular call when they were young boys. 'I think it was Bobby Charlton. Mum was ill at the time and Dad was chef. He was not very good at it and he was just doing us some boiled eggs. He was on the phone a long time and we noticed smoke coming out of the kitchen. The eggs were black in the pan and the water had all boiled off. Dad had to take us to the chippy.'

I thought I'd ring Jimmy again a couple of weeks before Christmas to wish him season's greetings.

'Fair,' he replied when I asked how he was. Rather than first lamenting the latest operation, that removal of a growth on the ear and the fifth operation in 12 months – 'they did it brilliantly' – he chose to bemoan his luck with his gas stove and gas fire that had broken down. 'I'm a thousand quid down,' he said. I couldn't help but smile. He told me to hang on a moment because Anne was doing the hoovering and he couldn't hear me properly.

'I do keep forgetting things,' he said. 'I can't write now, can't play the organ. I'm still trying to play the piano. I don't get bored though because I've always got something going wrong. We've got a Christmas tree upstairs that she wants to get down, but we're not sending Christmas cards this year. I hope people won't get upset.' I for one wouldn't, I said. They hoped to be going to John's for Christmas, he said. John was a deputy head, he told me, Duncan a manager in the NHS, pride in his voice. As there had been on other occasions when he'd told me the same things. So many calls did he get that he couldn't remember what he'd told to whom, I suspected. 'The boys have been very good,' he added.

'I can cope but it's hard. It's been a really trying time,' he said with his usual understatement. 'There's a stiffness in my neck all the time and it's very hard to sleep. Not slept properly for weeks, to be honest. I get a pain from the top of my chest to the bottom but it's most painful where the stitches have been. The neck is worst. Got three big lines on it.'

Watching football on television was still a consolation, he added, though the game 'is not as human as it was'. He still liked watching young players coming through, liked seeing players so fit and mobile these days. 'The coaching and training have improved so much. And the pitches,' he added. 'Every game is like the first game of August.' Still, there were elements that he wasn't enjoying: 'I wish they'd stop all this diving. I watch some games and I'm really disappointed. It's cheating. You never saw Tom Finney going down like that and they were always kicking him. But then, I suppose my generation will always find fault. My father did with my generation.' Then there was a pause, a wistfulness to his next comment: 'It would be interesting to play in it.'

He was tired, he said, and I didn't want to keep him on the phone any longer. I said the usual things, for him to take care of himself, that I hoped he felt better soon.

'Happy Christmas to you, Anne and the family. Hope to see you in the New Year,' were, I think, my last words to him.

8

I WAS writing something. I can't remember what, but I do remember that I was at the dining-room table on Monday, 22 January 2018 when I heard Vikki exclaim, 'Oh bloody hell. No,' from her office, before I heard her footsteps coming down the stairs as rapidly as the side effects of her heavy-duty cancer drugs would allow her.

'What's happened?' I asked.

'Jimmy's died,' she replied. She didn't even need to say which Jimmy, or from what context the Jimmy came.

I immediately felt shocked, then empty. I shed a tear. We shed a tear together. Gave each other a hug. Soon she was being asked by her sports desk to write Jim's obituary for *The Sun*. A very fine obit it would be too. I made tea. Walked around the house in a bit of a daze. I sort of knew it was coming, had been wondering if that call before Christmas might be our last, but still his death stunned. And still it hurt.

Not so much, clearly, as for the family. Duncan and John would tell me what that last Christmas and early New Year was like.

'The saddest period,' said Duncan.

'He'd been doing well but he started to go downhill in the first week of December,' said John. 'We took him to see the consultant from Preston, who came over to the Victoria because Dad couldn't make it over there. He'd got really thin again. His coat was too heavy for him. At home, he was mostly in his vest and braces.'

'He could barely lift his arms,' added Duncan. 'It was a struggle.'

In the end, they'd had to go to Jimmy and Anne's on Christmas Day, taking dinner with them, because their dad was unable to travel.

'He was in his pyjamas,' John recalled. 'He couldn't eat much. He said: "I've done my best." He wasn't well and he had a rash. We decided to call the doctor, who came out. He said Dad had shingles, on top of everything else.'

Still, Jimmy soldiered on into the New Year. 'What kept him alive was Mum being ill, I think,' said John. 'She was the love of his life and he wanted to stay with her.' Come mid-January, however, enough was enough. Jimmy needed full-time care. The choice was Trinity Hospice, where Jim had been president for 12 years. John drove him there, with Duncan following in his own car.

'He perked up when we got there,' John said. 'As I wheeled him in, he was jabbering away and he had a cup of tea and a piece of cake.'

Jimmy was set up on a morphine drip that released the painkiller automatically when required.

'All the pain went from his face and we were able to be with him over the next days,' John said. 'He died at 3am and we saw his last breath.'

I was sad for them, of course, as they both told me about Jimmy's final days. But I was pleased for them that their father was not in pain at the end and they were at his bedside, as I had been with my own father. To have been there at the end, I found, offers important solace in the years that come. And I was reminded of what Jimmy had told me in one of our last conversations over the last year: 'In the end, after everything you do in life, it's family that matter,' he said. 'The ones who'll be with you at the end.'

After this private death, the public reaction to it was remarkable and widespread. His successor as England captain, Bobby Moore, had died unbearably young, at the age of 51, of bowel cancer in 1993. It had shocked the nation. There was no shock now, given Jimmy's history of illness and him reaching 82 years of age, but there was sadness aplenty, in statements emanating from every nook and cranny of the football world and carried by every media outlet imaginable.

I wondered if Jimmy was the only footballer whose obituary appeared in both *The Times* and *Church Times*. The Rt Rev Geoffrey Pearson's for the latter was magnificent and one tale in it captured the essence of the man for me: 'I once invited him to speak at a men's breakfast organised in a small rural church,' wrote the Rev Pearson. 'He refused any fee, and there he met a young man, new to the Christian faith, who had brought his violin. Jimmy responded to the young man's request to play "Abide With Me". He waited until all had left, then slipped on to the organ seat and played. He then left the man with words of encouragement.'

I was writing very little for newspapers by now but, after my initial shock, I felt compelled to write about Jimmy, to say something via what I believe I do best. I phoned the new sports editor of my old paper the *Mail on Sunday*, Alison Kervin, and she agreed to carry a piece from me for the following week, recognising that the paper that had successfully campaigned to get him and 'my lot' World Cup medals should mark his passing appropriately.

A few days after the article appeared I found myself, as then vice-chairman of Salisbury FC, in front of an FA disciplinary panel containing former managers David Pleat and Gordon Milne, who had known Jimmy well from being professional players in his era. I was presenting our case concerning a series of on- and off-field episodes in a Southern League match that had caused an abandonment. David and Gordon complimented me on the piece and we reminisced about Jimmy before we all got down to business. Even so, to my chagrin, we were fined the same as the opposition, who were more culpable in my view. I'm sure that as an advocate – most of the time – for the old governing body, Jimmy would have been pleased to know that the FA's justice remained blind.

I so wanted to go to the funeral to pay my respects but didn't want to intrude on the family's grief nor burden them directly with a request that might embarrass them, knowing that St Peter's in Blackpool was not the biggest of churches and the number wanting to attend would be huge. Instead, I emailed Gordon Taylor. He replied to say he was indeed dealing with requests outside of the family, and from people in football, and space was to be allocated to close friends, in consultation with the family. He would get back to me. Word came a few days later that I was on the list of mourners.

I left for Blackpool before first light on the morning of Thursday, 8 February. I wanted to be there early for the 12.30pm service as I knew that parking in the streets off Lytham Road, along with seats in the church, would be at a premium. The weather worsened the further north I got. And I suddenly realised that, in my rush to get away early, I had forgotten my black tie. When I got to

Blackpool, the Tower barely visible through the mist, I headed for the Houndshill shopping centre to buy a new one. At the till, the woman asked me if it was for Jimmy Armfield's funeral. 'That's today, isn't it?' she asked rhetorically. I said it was. She told me she'd be thinking of his family.

The sea was battleship grey, the skies doom-laden dark as I parked down a side street of B&Bs near the church, a pebble's throw from Bloomfield Road. Inside, I found myself seated next to Warwick Rimmer, who had been Jimmy's centre-half when he was manager at Bolton Wanderers, and of whom he had written fondly in his autobiography. 'We always kept in touch,' said Warwick. 'We'd have a word now and then.' So many in this church did.

Across the aisle were Bobby and Jack Charlton, the latter with a copy of the *Daily Mirror* tucked under his arm and whose death due to dementia would occur two years after. Dotted about elsewhere were Trevor Brooking from the FA, Norman Hunter – that Prince Charming to Jimmy's panto narrator, and fellow 1966 squad member, who would himself pass a year later – from Leeds, along with Eddie

Gray. And of course, a liberal sprinkling of Jimmy's colleagues from BBC Radio 5 Live.

While we were all gathering, the funeral cortège took Jimmy on a final journey through Bloomfield Road, where several hundred fans had gathered to pay their respects at the passage of the coffin, which entered a corner of the ground and paused in front of the Armfield Stand before departing through another corner. On one side of the coffin was DAD in white carnations, inset with some tangerine roses; on the other side GRAMPS in a similar floral arrangement. Atop the casket was a beautiful mélange of England-shirt white lilies and roses. Elsewhere, at his statue, a wreath had been laid by the local NHS, for whom Jimmy had given much and from whom received so much in return.

We sang 'Now Thank We All Our God', 'The Lord's My Shepherd', 'Jerusalem' and the FA Cup Final hymn, 'Abide With Me'. For those who had grown up with the treasured old competition as a huge part of our lives, the singing of it evoked memories aplenty and barely suppressed tears. The four grandchildren read 'If' by Rudyard Kipling,

Jimmy's favourite poem, and Gordon Taylor delivered the most touching of tributes. Taylor has been a man often maligned, mostly and probably deservedly for his PFA salary of over £2 million a year. Today, however, he was at his best, eulogising a figure with whom he shared a deep love of the game. And all without notes.

'Jimmy's life was a social document,' he said, telling of how Jim had seen great change from the Second World War onwards and embraced it all, recognising and praising its enduring qualities rather than dwelling on and lamenting those it may have forgotten. Taylor grew emotional, with the rest of us, as he recalled this most upstanding of men. He told too of how Jimmy would often say he was retiring, and a farewell dinner would be arranged in his honour, only for him to arrive at the PFA offices in Manchester a day or two later wondering if there was anything he could do.

'I think that worked both ways,' Duncan later told me. 'I think Gordon would ring him up and ask him to come back because he liked to have him around.' I understood that. Jimmy's common-sense wisdom and general calm and reassuring presence would be invaluable to any organisation, not least that representing a profession he knew from top to bottom.

Duncan and John then combined to deliver the most beautiful and heartfelt eulogy to their father, both poignant and funny.

'Dad,' John said, 'was hard-working, selfless, strong, honest, kind, loving and gentle. He had no ego and always seemed, as he described, "happy with his lot". He was at total peace with himself and what he had done with his life, although in his final weeks he regretted not buying that new Mercedes or Jaguar.'

Duncan described his father as 'a modest man. He was showered with awards which he was deeply flattered by, but it never went to his head.'

They related how he told them whenever they had decisions to make that he would not be giving them advice, that they had to live their own lives and they needed to come to their own conclusions, before adding: 'But if I were you, what I would do is this...' Cue laughter.

Both Duncan and John told of a huge generosity of spirit, Jimmy passionate about young people getting chances in life, which was why he had been a school governor and proponent of Outward Bound. They also told a favourite story of mine about him, of how when they were boys, Jimmy would send them to Blackpool beach with buckets and spades not to play in the sand, but to follow the horses and donkeys to collect manure for his flower beds. And with strict instructions to get the 'fresh stuff. "There's nothing like the fresh stuff," he used to say. "And with no straw in it."'

It was a eulogy not about the landmark, high-achieving moments of Jimmy's life and its footballing greatness, for they had been well documented. This was about the intimacies of a father and his family, little things that you remember and that break your heart in the early recollections of grief before they return further down the road towards some kind of acceptance as comforting memories.

They talked of poking gentle fun at what he might be wearing, his insistence it was plenty good enough and he didn't need new (probably a legacy of the War generation's make-do-and-mend); his habit of turning down the offer of a cup of tea, then saying he would actually like 'half a cup' when beverages arrived for everyone else. 'It didn't mean any extra work for Mum as she would already have made it, knowing he would change his mind,' said John. Anne sat bereft in the front row, proud of her two boys doing their dad, her husband, proud. 'The glue that held the family together,' was the boys' consensus of her in their joint eulogy.

Most moving of all was Duncan's sharing of one of his final conversations with his father: 'A few weeks ago, he was lying in bed as he was unwell and I was with him,' he said. 'I was holding his hands and talking about the family and I think he knew at this stage that things were not great in terms of his health, so we discussed what lay ahead. All of a sudden he stopped, lifted his head up to look me in the eye and said: "You know, Duncan, I wish I could play football one more time."'

Anyone that hadn't so far 'gone', did now. Some of us looked down at the order of service, on the back page its crests of the Football Association, the Professional Footballers' Association and Blackpool FC, along with the Armfield family's own coat of arms, and a poem that spoke so eloquently:

Goodbye, my family, my life is past.
I loved you all to the very last.
Weep not for me, but courage take,
Love each other for my sake.
For those you love don't go away.
They walk beside you every day.

Weep not for me. As if anyone was going to obey that instruction. But there was something to make us smile as we departed into weather that mirrored our mood, the dark heavens weeping above the Fylde Coast. The parting music was so evocative of Jimmy, and the upbeat tone exactly what he would have wished: 'I Do Like to be Beside the Seaside', the eternal Radio 5 Live *Sports Report* theme (Da dum, da dum, da diddly dum) and, of course, the *Match of the Day* theme.

The coffin was then conveyed for a private family committal while the rest of us were invited for tea and sandwiches at Bloomfield Road. I gave it a miss. I'd had a four-hour drive up and faced another one back. Given my own cancer and the side effects of the drugs I was taking, I had to be careful not to get too tired and I didn't want to doze at the wheel. Besides, I wanted to be alone with my thoughts and memories. I was not really in the mood for conversation. And the day had made me want to be back with my Vikki as soon as I could. I knew our own time together was finite now – she had been told that her cancer had spread to her liver and so more chemotherapy loomed – though I didn't then quite realise how limited our time would be.

On the drive back, I thought of my local vicar who once wryly observed to me that he only ever buried saints, such was the frequent over-the-top outpouring of goodwill, and overlooking of shortcomings, accorded to the newly dead. But Jimmy transcended any such reservations.

(Later, I asked some people who knew him well if they had ever heard him swear. I know I hadn't. Neither had Duncan, even after that injustice with Leeds in the European Cup Final, he said. Mike Ingham had heard something in jest. In his book, he recalled being in Blackpool on holiday as a boy and was determined to get Jimmy's autograph as then England captain. He waited at Bloomfield Road one lunchtime and finally he saw Jimmy driving away from a different entrance to the one where he was standing. Mike ran, managed to get Jimmy to stop the car, and secured his signature. Years later, he told Jimmy the story. 'I was,' Jimmy replied with a smile, 'considering telling you to bugger off.')

Mostly, my thoughts on the journey home that day of the funeral were of a man whose sheer goodness and generosity of spirit were an example, to be cited when bad and ungenerous thoughts intruded. A man to make you a better person, to ask yourself: 'What would Jimmy do?' The memories were of a warm and convivial confidant and conversationalist, whose wisdom and wit – the former sagacious, the latter often unintentional – brought smiles to faces to mirror the broad, benign, gap-toothed one he frequently displayed.

Maya Angelou once wrote: 'I've learned that people will forget what you said, people will forget what you did, but people will never forget how you made them feel.' With Jimmy, I believed it went beyond that. I do remember what he said and I do remember what he did. I hear what she says about how he made me feel being most significant, however.

Jim's legacy would be secure, not just in hearts and minds but also tangibly beyond the statue of him that had been installed at Bloomfield Road in 2011. The year after his death, Duncan and John travelled to the England football headquarters at St George's Park in Staffordshire to open the newly named Jimmy Armfield Lecture Theatre. 'This all serves as a great reminder and a great comfort for the family to know that his name will always be kept alive,' said Duncan.

Then, in May 2021, just before England hosted the men's European Championships delayed by the pandemic, manager Gareth Southgate gave a marvellous interview to Matt Dickinson of *The Times*. In it, he cited Jimmy's example of selflessness in 1966 – epitomised in that picture of him in his red sweater beaming and congratulating Ramsey and Moore – as something that players of today, and certainly those in Southgate's squad, should seek to emulate. The greater good was what mattered, support for your colleagues.

And now, here in the present? Well, I lost my Vikki a year and two weeks after Jimmy died, following a final year almost as medically demanding and draining on her as was Jimmy's on him. I think often of that moment in Jim's hall after she'd walked slowly up the path and he'd given her a peck on both cheeks in welcome, having told me to fetch her from the car. And I think too of us wanting to see his World Cup winners' medal, which then didn't exist but whose eventual award came to cement a friendship between the three of us.

Duncan and John, meanwhile, continue to miss their father and to look out for Anne, whose own health began to deteriorate.

'We couldn't have wished for a better dad,' said Duncan. 'He left us with a thousand memories, not one of them bad.'

'He once told me, "All you need to do is devote yourself to your children,"' said John. 'And that's what he did for us.'

Football moves on apace, money for fees and wages ever more staggering despite the often challenging circumstances of its audience in straitened times, but I think Jimmy would have focused still on how the game has progressed for the better, always looking for the positive in such things as stadiums, pitches, training methods. I think he would still have been a top player in this era, able to adapt, as are all the greats. Remember that precocious teenaged right-back in Blackpool's first team believing he was helping out the double-marked Stanley Matthews with his innovative overlapping? Jim would have come through, all right.

Back in 1974, when Jimmy took over at Elland Road, inflation, strikes, an energy crisis and political turmoil enveloped the nation. Fast-forward to 2023 and inflation, strikes, an energy crisis and political turmoil have beset us all over again. We even had a Prime Minister who lasted just 44 days. Perhaps the similarities of the social and cultural backdrops are what drew me back to the curious, intriguing story of the Leeds United pantomime.

Actually, I think it was more than that, having begun to develop the idea for this book while still in the thick of my own painful loss. Writing it, wanting to honour an old friend, came only after my grief was beginning to abate. This book was perhaps most to do with needing to find goodness and hope in dark times, just as Leeds United FC did with Jim.

Social desperation is always around us, sadly, as revisiting Jimmy's life and story, his childhood informed by the Second World War, has shown. In two eras almost 50 years apart, cost-of-living issues highlight it more starkly. In both of them, through all the dark times, I like to think that Jim's beacon values, of respect and decency, will ever endure. Easy for some of us to say when choices for many between heating and eating can erode self-respect let alone respect for others. Without the example of people like Jimmy, however, it feels to me that we are lost. The trick I believe he revealed, as someone set above most people through talent and profile, is to remain among the rest of us but lift us by quiet example, one encounter at a time, in valuing that which is important – and that which is important is people.

Perhaps we will never see his like again in football – a rounded man who saw his religion, life and football as intertwined rather than separate – but we will always have his spirit to cling to and remind us. There is a speech in the film *Field of*

Dreams in which James Earl Jones, playing a writer named Terence Mann, speaks lyrically about the role of baseball in American life: 'This field, this game: it's a part of our past,' he says. 'It reminds us of all that once was good and could be again.'

In the middle of those sentiments can be found, and let us hope will ever be found, James Christopher Armfield, a man who reminded us of all that was good and could be again.

ABOUT THE AUTHOR

Pantomime Hero is Ian Ridley's 14th sports book. His previous works include the *Sunday Times* No.1 best-selling *Addicted*, written with the former Arsenal and England captain Tony Adams, which was shortlisted for the William Hill Sports Book of the Year award. The follow-up *Sober* was published in 2017, 20 years on. Three of his other books have also been nominated in the British Sports Book Awards.

His previous book, published by the Floodlit Dreams company he founded, was *The Breath of Sadness: On love, grief and cricket*, which is a moving account of coping with the death of his wife Vikki Orvice, a trailblazing sports journalist. It was also shortlisted for the William Hill Sports Book of the Year and called in by the PEN Ackerley Prize judges.

Over a 40-year career, Ian has been a sports writer for *The Guardian, The Daily Telegraph, The*

Observer and the *Mail on Sunday*, for whom he was Chief Football Writer. He was named Sports Journalist of the Year in the 2007 British Press Awards and shortlisted on two other occasions.

Ian has also written for television, including more than 20 episodes of the Sky One drama series *Dream Team*, and currently has a film script in development on the life story of the world champion boxer Darren Barker, based on the autobiography on which the two collaborated, *A Dazzling Darkness*.

In recent years, Ian has obtained a Masters degree in Crime and Thriller Writing at Cambridge University and turned his hand to fiction, writing two books in his Jan Mason investigative journalist series, *Outer Circle* and *Don't Talk*.

JANE PURDON

Jane is writing a passionate, heartfelt account of the summer of 2022, when the Lionesses dazzled the nation and brought football home. Alongside is her personal story of falling in love with the game aged seven and becoming an activist, administrator and leader, most recently as CEO of Women in Football.

Her journey takes in her early days as a Sunderland fan, her first kicks of a ball in her late teens, her pioneering work in the early 1990s to promote women's involvement in football, and her subsequent career at the heart of the football establishment. In 1992, Jane wrote: 'The England women's team winning the European Championship – now that is not a fairy tale, it could just happen'.

Thirty years later this fairy tale came true, and Jane reflects on what has happened to women's football in the aftermath of the Lionesses' historic victory, what needs to happen next, and looks forward to the FIFA Women's World Cup, taking place in the summer of 2023.

Publishes May 2023.

ANDY HAMILTON

Fans of the TV comedies *Drop the Dead Donkey* and *Outnumbered*, which Andy wrote with Guy Jenkin, will know what to expect from him – smart, funny and engaging. His memories of early football fandom and analysis of the modern game will be a similar treat.

Andy grew up a couple of streets from Stamford Bridge, and was taken to his first Chelsea game by his brother when aged six. Since then, he has seen everything – from erstwhile laughing stocks to Russian-moneyed dominance. And he has strong opinions on all of it.

Taking his starting point as a Chelsea v Newcastle United game back in the 1960s and ending up at a match between the two modern clubs now owned by Americans and Saudi Arabians respectively, this will be a read of warmth, wit and wisdom.

Publishes September 2023.

Visit www.football-shorts.co.uk for more information